Making Disciples, Making Leaders
Leader Guide

SECOND EDITION

Making Disciples, Making Leaders

Leader Guide

SECOND EDITION

A Manual for Presbyterian Church
Leader Development

Steven P. Eason
E. Von Clemans

WESTMINSTER
JOHN KNOX PRESS
LOUISVILLE • KENTUCKY

First edition published 2004. Second edition 2016, 2022

Second edition
Published by Westminster John Knox Press
Louisville, Kentucky

22 23 24 25 26 27 28 29 30 31—10 9 8 7 6 5 4 3 2

Book design by Sharon Adams
Cover design by Allison Taylor

Library of Congress Cataloging-in-Publication Data is on file at the Library of Congress, Washington, DC.

ISBN-13: 978-0-664-26676-9

Most Westminster John Knox Press books are available at special quantity discounts when purchased in bulk by corporations, organizations, and special-interest groups. For more information, please e-mail SpecialSales@wjkbooks.com.

*We are grateful to the ruling elders and deacons
with whom we have had the pleasure of serving in ordered ministry.
Their corrections, suggestions, and feedback over the years have
refined this leadership development model into the useful tool it is today.
They have shown us again and again when you ask for a lot, you get a lot.
Their willingness to respond to God's call and their effectiveness
as spiritual leaders in the Church proves the effort needed
to develop spiritual leaders is worth it. It has been a team effort,
and we as pastors and the Church have benefited.
We dedicate this book to all of you with deep appreciation.*

Contents

Acknowledgments

*O*ur thanks go to the leadership and members of Myers Park Presbyterian Church, Charlotte, North Carolina. They have graciously encouraged and supported our work on this project through the years and have understood the value of sharing our efforts with the larger Church.

We are especially grateful to Katie Brigulio, our administrative assistant, who at the eleventh hour bailed us out by collating and preparing our manuscripts for submission.

Introduction

*I*n our seminars throughout the country, we have asked teaching elders, ruling elders, and deacons "What has changed around the church in the past twenty years?" The answer: everything!

- youth sports on Sunday
- blue laws
- declining membership
- decreasing budgets
- aging church members
- dual career families
- increasing biblical illiteracy
- higher divorce rates
- removal of prayer in schools
- technology and communication
- more church scandals
- lack of trust in institutions
- growing secularism
- increased mobility
- the death of "American Christendom"

Wow! Is that all?

Who is leading the Church? Where are they leading it? How will they get there? What is being done in leadership development? Why make this a priority when there is a so much more to do?

Three-fourths (77 percent) of PC(USA) churches have two hundred or fewer members. More than half (55 percent) have one hundred or less (https://www.presbyterianmission.org/ministries/research/10faq/).

So it stands to reason most sessions are small. That means there are very few people within those small congregations from whom to choose deacons and ruling elders. The same few people rotate on and off the session or dia-conate. So why do any training? They've all been there before and know what to do. Run the church, run the committees, raise the money, set the budget—but is there more?

When we ask Presbyterian ministers around the country what they are cur-rently doing in training newly elected deacons and ruling elders, the number one answer is "Nothing!" That is followed by "Very little." Rarely have we found someone who has made this a priority in their ministry. We're curious as to why.

There are hundreds of books available on leadership development, but what we offer is leadership development within the church. We propose a shift from perfunctory management to spiritual leadership, from information to formation, from membership to discipleship. We provide an assortment of tools for developing leaders who can:

- grow in their own faith and discipleship
- function as a team with clergy
- cultivate and equip members of the congregation to be in ministry
- have a working knowledge of "the Presbyterian way"
- gain a functional understanding of Reformed theology
- know what business the church is in and be good at that business

These types of leaders do not fall out of the sky. Just because they are leaders in business, education, health care, government, or the judicial sys-tem does not mean they will be effective leaders in the church. Anyone can manage a church with budgets, buildings, programs, and staff; but leadership in the church is first and foremost about discipleship with Christ.

We offer more than a training program for newly elected deacons and rul-ing elders. This system of leadership cultivation is interrelated, ongoing, and can be designed for any size congregation. All churches need leadership. You can custom fit our resources to your current situation.

Teaching elders have an opportunity here to teach. Rather than clergy functioning as the "church chaplain," they can develop a team to join them in ministry. This model treats ruling elders and deacons as colleagues rather than employees or volunteers. This is an intentional move from a "member-ship model" to a "discipleship model." This will expand your vision from management to leadership.

When we made this shift, ruling elders and deacons completed their terms with comments such as: "I'm going to miss the fellowship and being on the team." That's a huge shift. But this isn't magic; it's hard work. It takes years of being consistent and committed. You are raising the bar. Expect some resistance. The payoff is worth the effort.

Chapter 1 provides biblical principles for leadership development in the church. Chapter 2 puts the spotlight on the Nominating Committee. Choosing good leaders is half the battle. Chapter 3 lays out the framework of our training model.

Chapter 4 explores strategies and activities for teaching in light of recent research on the brain. Chapter 5 argues for worship as a foundation for Christian leadership development. Chapter 6 gives you options to design a course that will work for you.

Chapter 7 explains "The Orientation Meeting" and provides helpful tips for setting up your course. Chapters 8–11 outline our four-part workshop model for training.

The Presbyterian Church (U.S.A.) is in the middle of approving an additional confession to the *Book of Confessions*. The 221st General Assembly (2014) sent a proposed amendment to the Presbyterian Church (U.S.A.)'s *Book of Confessions* that would add the Belhar Confession, which has its roots in the struggle against apartheid.

Before it can be added to the denomination's confessions, the Belhar first had to be ratified by 115, or two-thirds, of the denomination's 171 presbyteries. It easily succeeded being approved in 2014–2015. A new confession must be approved by two successive General Assemblies, and so the final step in the adoption of the Belhar Confession will be decided in the 222nd General Assembly in the summer of 2016. There are many resources available for study of this confession on the denomination's website. If and when it is adopted, this book will be updated to reflect the new confession.

Chapter 12 provides a structure and suggestions for conducting the session examinations of new leaders. Chapter 13 invites you to evaluate and possibly renovate your current session or deacon meetings. Why do a great job at training to bring leaders onto an inefficient council? Chapter 14 offers other opportunities for leadership development beyond the training program.

This book can be either a resource to enhance the good things you are already doing or a radical shift in the way you cultivate leadership within your church. Either way, its an effective tool.

Every church in America is facing significant changes in our culture. Those changes affect the church. How will the church affect culture? That's a question for leadership.

Chapter 1

Biblical Principles for Church Leadership

According to Genesis 2:18, the only thing in all of creation that was "not good" was that humanity was alone—disconnected, isolated, having no one to share the burdens and joys of life. Even God apparently does not enjoy working alone. God chooses to work with folk like us. Think of the great leaders of the Bible: Abram, Sarai, Moses, Gideon, David, Mary Magdalene, and Simon Peter. None of these were exactly star players, but God chose to work with them, which is no small detail. When we work alone, it's not good. Even God chooses to work on a team!

Leadership in the Old Testament

Perhaps the most prominent example of team ministry within the Old Testament is that found in the account of Jethro's advice to Moses:

> [14]"Why do you sit alone, while the people stand around you from morning until evening? . . . [18]You will surely wear yourself out. . . . For the task is too heavy for you; you cannot do it alone. . . . [21]You should also look for able [people] . . . who fear God, are trustworthy, and hate dishonest gain; set such [people] over them as officers over thousands, hundreds, fifties and tens. . . . [22]So it will be easier for you, and they will bear the burden with you. If you do this, and God so commands you, then you will be able to endure." (Exod. 18:14, 18, 21, 22–23)

It is not good to "sit alone" (v. 14). How many clergy, ruling elders, or deacons do you think are "sitting alone," or feel they are? According to clergy burnout statistics, the percentage is pretty high. If the goal, as Jethro states it, is "to endure" (v. 23), then leadership has to be shared. That's the "Jethro Principle."

The Jethro Principle does not really belong to Jethro. His comment to Moses was, "If you do this, and God so commands" (v. 23). The implication is that God has observed Moses operating in solo fashion and has assessed that this leadership style cannot provide what is necessary. Thus God instituted shared leadership and team ministry as a provision of grace. The alternative was for Moses to continue operating alone and "wear [him]self out" (v. 18a). The apparent motive behind Jethro's (and God's) advice was to ward off failure, to secure success. A record of Moses's prayer reveals his frustration and hopelessness in operating alone:

> [10]Moses heard the people weeping throughout their families, all at the entrances of their tents. Then the LORD became very angry, and Moses was displeased. [11]So Moses said to the LORD, "Why have you treated your servant so badly? Why have I not found favor in your sight, that you lay the burden of all this people on me? Did I conceive all this people? Did I give birth to them, that you should say to me, 'Carry them in your bosom, as a nurse carries a sucking child,' to the land that you promised on oath to their ancestors? . . . [14]I am not able to carry all this people alone, for they are too heavy for me. [15]If this is the way you are going to treat me, put me to death at once—if I have found favor in your sight—and do not let me see my misery." (Num. 11:10–12, 14–15)

This is a "Kill Me Prayer!" In other words, "I'd rather be dead than to be in ministry this way." Many a person has prayed this prayer.

Moses prayed, and God responded. Rather than kill Moses, God directed him to recruit seventy of the ruling elders of Israel and bring them to the tent of meeting, where God would do the rest:

> I will take some of the spirit that is on you and put it on them; and they shall bear the burden of the people along with you so that you will not bear it all by yourself. (Num. 11:17)

God empowers leadership, but we have to get to the tent of meeting. We have to position ourselves for empowerment. Empowerment is not a program or even a training course. It's a gift from God. Though we cannot achieve it, we do need to receive it. Our posture for receptivity is critical.

The team was empowered together. God didn't select the seventy and empower them in the privacy of their homes. Moses selected the seventy, and God empowered them with the spirit at the tent of meeting—together, in one place. Leadership is communal. By God's design, human leadership is recruited and equipped to participate with God in the task of leading and guiding the people. God's covenant with Abraham was a sharing of leadership. Israel's history of judges, kings, and prophets reflects God's choice to work with others toward the common goal of retrieving a lost humanity. In the Old Testament, God clearly chooses not to act alone, and God does not intend for human leadership to act alone either.

Leadership in the New Testament

If I had been Jesus, I would have definitely chosen to work alone! The disciples seem to have been in the way. But God chooses to work on a team, even if, and perhaps especially when, the team is dysfunctional. There's hope for any session!

Christ called twelve students. He intentionally recruited each one of them. All of them were busy. None of them had previous skills in being a leader in the church. They weren't volunteers. They were disciples, students, people going to school to obtain skill and knowledge. They weren't clergy. Jesus took fishermen, tax collectors, political activists, and businessmen to build his team. He took people with the potential for learning. He saw that potential in them and called it forth, even when they didn't see it themselves. Jesus charged the twelve with the task of leading the church, but always in the context of partnership with him.

> "Go therefore and make disciples of all nations, baptizing them . . . and teaching them to obey everything that I have commanded you. And remember, I am with you always." (Matt. 28:19–20)

A prime example of the team ministry philosophy of Christ is found within the story of the feeding of the five thousand (Mark 6:30–44). Jesus has taken the disciples away to rest, but, when they get out of the boat, they are met with more demands and needs. The disciples immediately draw up a plan to dismiss the crowds because of the late hour and the probability that food could be found in nearby villages.

Note Jesus' response to their plan: "You give them something to eat" (Mark 6:37a). Everyone sees the obvious impossibility of this task. Nevertheless, Jesus puts the privilege of ministry on the twelve. They respond with apparent sarcasm: "Are we to spend a year's salary on this group?' (v. 37). Jesus replies: "How many loaves have you? Go and see" (v. 38). Jesus looks to them to provide the base resources from which a miracle will grow.

Once they surrender their meager resources—five loaves and two fish—to Christ, it is by the power of God that provisions are made for the five-thousand-plus people who are present. Christ takes the resources, looks beyond the human realm to heaven, and then "bless[es] and [breaks] the loaves" (v. 41a); but the twelve gathered the resources in the first place.

Notice Jesus' next move. He gives the multiplied fish and loaves "to his disciples to set before the people" (6:41b). Jesus uses the disciples, in team fashion, to serve the people. Again, he pulls his followers into the experience. Jesus' floating the food out to the folk would have been quicker and more impressive. Using human resources took a lot longer, but the disciples/students would have missed the experience had he not.

When all had eaten, they took up twelve baskets of leftovers. That's one basket per disciple. Their own personal needs were provided for in abundance, just as they provided for others. But Jesus makes number thirteen on the team. The others had to feed him out of their own baskets. Imagine that!

Some may read this story and marvel at the ability of Jesus to multiply fish. An underlying and perhaps more significant lesson is revealed if you watch the interrelatedness of Christ with the world (the five thousand), with his disciples, and the disciples with the world. The story begs us to ask of ourselves: *What are our resources? What do we have to offer that Christ can use?*

Implications for the Presbyterian Church (U.S.A.)

As Presbyterians, we ordain people to the ordered ministries of deacon and ruling elder. They are called to ministry. We lay hands on them. They take vows. We are a team by God's design. It is a gift! We need to utilize it. Working alone is neither biblical nor effective. Working on a team is energizing and life-giving. It's a gift!

Chapter 2

Choosing the Team—
The Nominating Committee

*W*ho in our churches is qualified to serve as deacons and ruling elders? Getting the right people is half the battle. What if we took the nominating process more seriously? Here's the kind of people who need to serve:

> To those called to exercise special functions in the church—deacons, ruling elders, and teaching elders—God gives suitable gifts for their various duties. In addition to possessing the necessary gifts and abilities, those who undertake particular ministries should be persons of strong faith, dedicated discipleship, and love of Jesus Christ as Savior and Lord. Their manner of life should be a demonstration of the Christian gospel in the church and in the world. They must have the approval of God's people and the concurring judgment of a council of the church. *(Book of Order, G-2.0104a)*

That's a tall order—for all of us. Without God empowering us with the Holy Spirit, none of us is qualified to serve any ministry within the church. Yet flawed as we may be, we are called to service. Incredible!

There is a human dimension to the call process. You, like Moses, are charged to choose the people whom you deem to be qualified to serve. How are you doing that? We have found that most churches spend very little time in the nominating process. A committee is formed, names are collected, candidates are chosen, calls are made, and the slate is submitted to the congregation. That's about it. Would we get better results if we did more?

Strengthening the Nominating Process

Do you nominate, elect, train, and ordain in the fall of the year and install the new class in January? There are pros and cons to that timeframe. Here's another option.

September to December is packed with activities in most churches. There are fall start-ups, the stewardship campaign, budget setting, Thanksgiving, Advent, and Christmas. Add weddings, funerals, baptisms, presbytery meetings, and you get the picture. Fall is a cluttered time to be nominating, electing, and training leaders. Not to mention, in January you're changing the guard right in the middle of your program year.

What if you were to change the terms of service to begin in June? Now you can elect leaders at a January congregational meeting, train them during February–April, examine them and celebrate an ordination/installation service in May, and they begin their term June 1. You move it out of the clutter and end the "fruit-basket turnover" in the middle of your busiest season.

To make this shift, your current outgoing class will need to serve five more months (January–May). When we made the change, some in that class could not continue through May, so we simply left those seats open. It's a brief transition time. Changing your class terms, the work of the Nominating Committee could follow this pattern:

January

The Nominating Committee is elected at the congregation's annual meeting.

February

First meeting: Do a Bible study using our chapter on "A Biblical Model for Team Leadership." Read Exodus 18:17–18, 22–33; Numbers 11:10–12, 14–15, Ephesians 4:11–16. Discuss some of the following questions together:

1. Why do you think God would choose to use humans in shared leadership?
2. How would you compare what we look for in ruling elders/deacons with what God asked Moses to look for in choosing his team? (see Num. 11:10–12, 14–15)
3. Do you feel we are calling people to ministry, or are we just filling slots?

Allow time for the group to grasp the significance of their work. Train the Nominating Committee! Give them articles to read. Pray with them. Again, we are "teaching elders." We need to teach!

April–May

Use a process to solicit names from the congregation during April and May, before the summer break. At first, this will seem way to early. Election is not until next January! Hang with it. It's helpful to have a form for the congregation to use in submitting their nominees. (See Appendix 1: Leader Nomination Form.) This standardizes the process for the committee.

In April: We have the Nominating Committee attend a session and diaconate meeting in order to see the work in progress. They get to see the group to which they are nominating folks to serve. What is the balance of men and women? What is the age distribution?

Study the outgoing classes. Are we losing our chair of finance? What gifts and skills will we need? Are we losing our youth chair or clerk of session? Representation is important along with needed gifts and skills. Where are the holes going to be and who can fill them?

In May: Distribute copies of "Everything You Ever Wanted to Know about Elders and Deacons" to the Nominating Committee (see the *Participant Workbook*). Have them answer the true/false questions (make it an open book test). Then go through each question together, hearing responses and giving the correct answers (see answer key in appendix 2).

As a part of their orientation, review any Nominating Committee policies your church may have. Review the schedule and timeline and answer any questions.

Distribute copies of G-2.01–2.04 from the *Book of Order*. These sections deal with the call, gifts and qualifications, definition of the ministry, preparation, and service of ordination and installation. Discuss.

June

The June meeting of the Nominating Committee can be devoted to reviewing the congregation's recommendations. Before that list makes it to the Nominating Committee, we send it to the church treasurer or business administrator. Are these nominees faithful stewards? This gets sticky, but consider what you are doing if you elect someone who is not a faithful steward. "Faithful steward" is not defined by dollar amount but by giving history. How could a nominee make decisions about the finances and priorities of the church if they do not personally give? Again, amount is not the issue—faithful giving history is the standard for leadership. The revised list is then given to the Nominating Committee. The committee now has time to cull through the list of names.

July–August

Take July off. A meeting in August needs to be dedicated to working the names down to first, second, and third choices. If you need a ruling elder to oversee the Finance Committee, have two or three choices lined up, in case of refusals. Work the list.

September–October

Now is the time to call on your first choices. We suggest face-to-face contacts. No phone calls. This communicates the importance of the decision. It is helpful to prepare a "call packet" with information about training, meetings, expectations, terms of ministry, ordination/installation, and other pertinent information to the call.

In appendix 3 you will find sample copies of letters we provide for the nominees. They actually sign these and return them to us.

November–December

Once you have received the acceptance from all nominees, you can present the slate to the session—for information only. They have no vote or input as to who is nominated, but we do this as a courtesy. The session will call the Congregational Meeting on a designated date in January (we do ours on a Sunday morning) for the purpose of electing a new class of deacons and ruling elders.

The Nominating Committee has done its work! How different is that from pulling a group together in the fall and rushing to get some names? It takes time to identify and call quality leaders, whether you are in a small, medium, or large congregation. This matters and can help set the pace for building a strong leadership team.

We've included a copy of our Nominating Committee Policies in appendix 4. This is a valuable asset to our committee. It was drafted by a task force chaired by the clerk of session and then approved by the congregation at one of its annual meetings. It provides clear guidance and boundaries for our Nominating Committee and may be useful to yours.

Chapter 3

Making Leaders—What to Teach

*I*n order to prepare effective leaders for your church, you need to be clear about what such a leader needs to know and how such a leader would function.

Our *Book of Order* provides only general guidance about the content and process. In G-2.0402 we read:

> When persons have been elected to the ordered ministry of ruling elder or deacon, the session shall provide a period of study and preparation, after which the session shall examine them as to their personal faith; knowledge of the doctrine, government, and discipline contained in the Constitution of the church; and the duties of the ministry. The session shall also confer with them as to their willingness to undertake the ministry appropriate to the order. If the examination is approved, the session shall appoint a day for the service of ordination and installation.

Apart from the individual's willingness to serve in ordered ministry, it is only the end result that is specified—each leader shall be examined and approved in five areas:

- Personal faith
- Knowledge of the doctrine of the church
- Knowledge of the government of the church
- Knowledge of the discipline of the church
- The duties of the ministry

Implicit in the subsequent required ordination/installation service is also the leader's willingness to affirmatively answer the nine constitutional questions for ordination and installation found in W-4.0404.

Before we look at these content areas more closely, we need to think about the difference between making leaders who can answer questions and those who can function as spiritual leaders in your congregation.

Information vs. Formation

All of us have lots on our plates—pastors, leaders, and leaders-elect. The great temptation is to avoid doing the difficult work of developing the personal faith of incoming leaders and to focus on covering the more objective framework and facts of the constitution. A single class introducing the *Book of Order* and *Book of Confessions* may seem adequate. Perhaps several classes covering the major parts of the constitution seems sufficient. A perfunctory examination gets warm bodies into needed leadership positions.

If there is a deficiency in the lay leadership of today's church, if there is a lack of spiritual maturity among many who would serve as ruling elders and deacons, can that deficiency be addressed by finding better ways to put more facts and information into the minds of church leaders? Will being able to quote chapter and verse from the *Book of Order* or the *Book of Confessions* make individuals better leaders in the church? Better disciples? Can the recital of the details of Presbyterian polity or the doctrines of Reformed theology ever compensate for an under-developed personal faith? No.

What this model of leadership development does is to understand the development of the leader's personal faith as *the* business of the church and the absolutely essential prerequisite for faithful and effective leadership in the church.

Therefore, a great deal of the leader development process in this model is designed to nurture and develop each leader's personal faith. Corporate worship begins every time we gather, grounding us in shared faith through Scripture. The sharing of personal faith experiences in small groups binds leaders into a community of faith that recognizes individual variety, yet one common witness. Sharing a meal together joins us in the sacred tradition of food feeding faith.

Spiritual formation is at the center of this model, not instilling information. So, if some is good, isn't more better? Why not eliminate all the content and focus solely on spiritual formation, on just developing personal faith?

One reason is found in our constitution. Personal faith is but one of five areas in which leaders are to be examined. Our constitution requires that leaders demonstrate a satisfactory working knowledge of the doctrine, government, and discipline of the church, and the duties of the ordered ministry of ruling elder and deacon.

Another reason is located in our identity as Presbyterians. If we focused entirely on personal faith development, we might end up with highly developed spiritual persons, but they wouldn't necessarily be Presbyterian leaders of Presbyterian congregations.

The Challenge of Presbyterian Identity

In the spring of 2018, the Presbyterian Church (U.S.A.) published the *Religious and Demographic Profile of Presbyterians 2015*. (To see the full report, go to www.pcusa.org and search for "Presbyterian Panel.") Over 2,400 members and ministers were part of a Presbyterian panel assembled to give a snapshot of who makes up the Presbyterian Church (U.S.A.). Over half (53 percent) of members were not raised in Presbyterian churches. The average length of membership in their current congregation was twenty years.

This means that, unless your congregation chooses only born-and-bred Presbyterians as leaders, more than half of your leaders will have been something other than Presbyterian previously. Most of our ruling elders and deacons come into leadership roles with little understanding of the Presbyterian Church (U.S.A.)—what it stands for and how it works—or only what they pick up through observation and osmosis.

If the Presbyterian Church (U.S.A.) has anything valuable or distinctive to offer to Christians in the twenty-first century, its leaders will need to have a working knowledge of the specific beliefs and behaviors that make us who we are as Presbyterians.

Finding Balance

We must attend to both formation *and* information. We contend that much of traditional leader development has focused on information. We need to raise the level of spiritual formation of leaders to balance information about the Presbyterian Church (U.S.A.). Properly framed, information about the church can be a means of spiritual formation.

In our recommended model, we will focus on the spiritual formation of persons with a personal relationship to Jesus Christ as Lord *and* on providing leaders with the information needed to serve as effective Presbyterian ruling elders and deacons. We will lean heavily on experiences and activities that foster personal spiritual growth. But we will also make sure each leader will be able to articulate not only personal faith but also their knowledge of the doctrine, government, and discipline of the church as well as the duties of his or her particular ministry and be able to answer the constitutional questions with integrity and enthusiasm. Along the way they will experience and learn how to do ministry as a team of spiritual leaders.

Constitutional Questions as Framework

The constitutional questions asked of all persons being ordained or installed to ordained ministry effectively balance the twin goals of spiritual leadership and a working familiarity with Presbyterian polity. If you lay the constitutional questions alongside the five content areas required in the examination ordination/installation, you can see the balance. (See the *Participant Workbook*, Supplemental Resources, "Constitutional Questions for Ordination and Installation: Content Areas," p. 45.)

Here is another way to see the correlation:

Personal Faith

Question a. Do you trust in Jesus Christ your Savior . . .?

Question f. Will you in your own life seek to follow the Lord Jesus Christ . . .?

Question g. Do you promise to further the peace, unity, and purity of the Church?

Question h. Will you pray for and seek to serve the people with energy, intelligence, imagination, and love?

Doctrine

Question b. Do you accept the Scriptures . . .?

Question c. Do you sincerely receive and adopt the essential tenets of the Reformed faith?

Question d. Will you fulfill your ministry in obedience to Jesus Christ, under the authority of Scripture, and be continually guided by our Confessions?

Governance and Discipline

Question e. Will you be governed by our church's polity and abide by its discipline?

Question i. (ruling elders) Will you share in government and discipline . . .?

Duties of the Ordered Ministry

Question i. (ruling elders) Will you . . . [watch] over the people, providing for their worship, nurture, and service . . . serving in the councils of the church . . . try to show the love and justice of Jesus Christ?

Question i. (deacons) Will you . . . teaching charity, urging concern, and directing the people's help to the friendless and those in need . . . try to show the love and justice of Jesus Christ?

Any leader who understands what is at stake in the constitutional questions and can answer them with integrity and enthusiasm will be a leadership asset to your church. Helping you develop such leaders is the goal of this book.

Chapter 4

Making Leaders—How to Teach

*I*n the last chapter, we looked at the balance of information and formation an effective Presbyterian leader will need. Now we turn to the other primary component. In order for spiritual formation to be an outcome of this development model, we need to pay as much attention to *process* as we do to the content. Spiritual leadership will be formed through the experience of each leader in all the various activities, interactions with other leaders, moments of worship, opportunities for quiet reflection, and building relationships with the pastor(s) and leaders of the congregation. *How* we help people know and understand the things leaders need to know will shape the kind of leaders they will become.

In the following sections, we will provide an overview of the basic educational assumptions upon which the learning activities are based. First, we will look at the conditions under which adult learners learn best. Then we will review some of the current research on the human brain and explore the implications of those findings for our purposes. Finally, we will make suggestions for making the physical environment more conducive to a great learning experience.

Adult Learners

There has been a great deal of research on how adults learn. Certain conditions provide the optimal experience for adult learners.

The following is list of these conditions and some implications for developing leaders in the Church. The list is adapted from *The Kerygma Program Guide* (Frank Bates and Barbara Minges, *The Kerygma Program: Ideas, Perspectives, and Strategies for Planning Effective Adult Education in the Church* [Pittsburgh, PA: The Kerygma Program, 1990], 13).

Adults learn best and are most involved when they:

- **Are responsible for their own learning**—Learners are not dependent upon the leader as the only expert, authority, and primary source of information.
  - In this model, we will assume each leader is intelligent and capable of, individually and with others, finding factual answers in and discerning meaning from resource material. Pastors/leaders should resist being resident experts; instead, they should empower learners with the tools and confidence to find answers on their own. The leader does not have to be a content expert or an accomplished spiritual director. A pastor or leader does have to be willing to let go of any need to be the expert so that learners can take responsibility for their own learning.
- **Can participate directly in the process of their own learning**—Learners make decisions about what and how they will learn, and interact with the subject matter and other learners.
  - Learners should have opportunities, within the overall structure, to make decisions about what, when, and how they will learn. Leaders provide multiple approaches and activities for learners—something as simple as "choose one of these three tasks"—and learners regularly choose from among options.
- **Are treated as individuals in a setting where differences are valued and respected**—Learners should be exposed to a variety of teaching/learning styles and encouraged to work at their own pace and make applications that are appropriate to them.
  - Respect for each learner, at all levels of experience, knowledge, and maturity, will be paramount. Leaders provide and nurture a learning environment where the expression of and acceptance of differences is expected and encouraged. Leaders will intervene if needed to protect each individual's dignity.
- **Have opportunity to practice skills and express ideas and learning in their own words**—Learners will express insights and interpretations in their own words and not be expected to repeat rote responses.
  - Presentation of content is never complete until learners are encouraged to reflect upon their opinions/responses and then share them with others.
- **Are within an environment of trusting relationships**—Learners are helped to become caring and supportive of other learners, and are encouraged to share feelings, needs, concerns, as well as information and ideas.
  - Leaders model by example the kind of relationships they desire among the learners and create an atmosphere of openness to each

individual's perspective. Leaders gently guide the group in maintaining a supportive environment.

- **Are not in competition with other learners**—Learners' motivation comes through activities and resources that facilitate a cooperative, collaborative style of learning.
  - Learners will work in groups to discuss individual learning and questions. Activities are designed to foster a collaborative or team approach to assignments, tasks, and projects.
- **Are exposed to strategies that enhance a person's self-worth**—Persons with a positive self-concept are less threatened by new information and experiences.
  - Learning activities are designed not to embarrass or highlight lack of knowledge or experience. Leaders encourage each learner and find something of value in each learner comment, response, or question. Leaders model the kind of person/leader they hope learners will become.
- **Gain a sense of satisfaction and experience success in the process of their learning.**
  - Teaching strategies and activities are designed so that learners can and do achieve satisfaction and success instead of experiencing frustration. Too much frustration inhibits learning. Make sure every learner becomes a valued participant.

The role of the pastor/leader is like that of a coach dedicated to the growth and improvement of the team.

Brain Research and Learning

John Medina, a developmental molecular biologist and research consultant, wrote a book entitled *Brain Rules: 12 Principles for Surviving and Thriving at Work, Home, and School* (Seattle, WA: Pear Press, 2008). He lays out twelve rules that explain how our brains work. Taking each rule seriously will shape how we teach and suggest practical strategies to apply in our learning environments.

Rule #1: Exercise boosts brain power.

If the brain is built for our bodies to change, and physical exercise is food for the brain, then the absolute worst thing we can do is to remain stationary.

- Introduce some kind of movement in each class segment or at least every hour: stand up, move around, wave hands, talk to someone across the room, try classroom "aerobic" exercises.
- If you sense energy is depleted, use movement to re-energize.
- No more hour-long sessions of just talking/listening/viewing.

Rule #2: The human brain evolved, too.

If the evolution of the brain has created a heightened sensitivity to threats to our survival and a bias toward cooperation as a means of managing those threats, then safety—physical and relational—in the classroom is a primary concern.

- Focus on the quality of your relationships to students.
- Focus on creating a safe and hospitable environment for learning.
- Protect students' integrity, actively intervening if necessary.
- Encourage articulation of fears and threats.
- Invite students to help shape the classroom to be more hospitable.

Rule #3: Every brain is wired differently.

If every person's brain is unique, then treating everyone the same dishonors those we teach.

- Remind yourself before every class that *every* student brings a unique and valuable perspective into the classroom.
- Be aware of appropriate and realistic expectations.
- Aim for smaller, rather than larger, class groups for optimal interaction for learning. (A group size of five to eight is best.)
- Allow students to follow their own paths as much as possible.
- Use insights from multiple intelligences to provide a variety of activities. (see Bradley J. Wigger, *Multiple Intelligences: Understanding the Many Ways We Learn*, available free through www.thethoughtfulchristian .com.)
- Encourage students to select from a range of activity choices so they can choose what suits them.
- Encourage students to use the tools (intelligences) that work best for them.

Rule #4: We don't pay attention to boring things.

If the brain can focus on only one thing at a time (no multitasking) and emotions help to sharpen that focus, then the teacher's role is to make the classroom exciting and "charged."

- Keep it simple: instructions, questions, directions.
- Set ten minutes as a limit for "presenting" material. Take breaks to tell a story or provide an emotionally charged narrative, activity, or example.
- Provide big picture or main thought first and then elaborate with specifics. Start with meaning before details.
- Develop a repertoire of "hooks" and illustrations to use as transitions.
- Talk about and share what is known about the way the brain works.
- Focus on one thing at a time.

Rule #5: Repeat to remember.

If the brain's encoding of new information is enhanced by the immediate environment in which that information is received, then we must attend to the *way* we present as well as *what* we present.

- Help students remember specific information by using the same environment each time it is presented.
- Encourage "context-dependent" learning.
- Find ways to elaborately encode information when presented for memorization. Have learners come up with their own mantra, mnemonic, or memory aid.
- Use lots of examples.
- Focus on making really good introductions.
- Encourage students to first find meaning before committing to memory.

Rule #6: Remember to repeat.

If memory is not fixed at the moment of learning, and repetition provides the fixative, then teachers must continually reinforce previous learning through multiple restatements over time.

- Build review into every lesson.
- Revisit previously covered content at intervals to reinforce it.
- Information must be revisited for it to "stick." Cramming is not a strategy for the long term.
- To retain better, space out initial exposure and reviews of topics.

Rule #7: Sleep well, think well.

If the brain requires adequate sleep to function at its best, then attention to our own and our student's sleep patterns will be of great personal and classroom benefit.

- Make sure you get enough sleep! Encourage learners to do so.
- Be attentive to scheduling issues with respect to individual body rhythms (not too early or too late in the day).
- Build in some quiet time for relaxation and reflection.

Rule #8: Stressed brains don't learn the same way.

If brains and bodies under stress have difficulty learning, then reducing the stressors in the classroom and being aware of external stressors will make for a better learning environment.

- Find healthy ways to manage your stress. Have learners share what works for them.
- Notice how stress affects our bodies and watch for signs in students.
- Give choices to students as one way of giving them control.
- Work on empowering and encouraging students in multiple ways.

Rule #9: Stimulate more of the senses.

If the brain learns best when we stimulate multiple senses with multiple cues at the same time, then classrooms must be multisensory experiences.

- Use different senses to introduce/review the same material. (There are more senses than sight and sound.)
- Try to involve as many senses simultaneously as possible.

Rule #10: Vision trumps all other senses.

If vision is the dominant sense and trumps all others, then pictures and images should be more prominent than words.

- Use fewer words and more images, especially in presentations.
- Make use of image animation and presentation programs.
- Video clips can be more powerful than still images.
- Use color and movement.

Rule #11: Male and female brains are different.

If gender differences in the brain mean there are gender differences in how we respond and function, then being aware and appreciative of those differences is necessary for effective teaching and learning.

NOTE: Medina observes that while there are genetic, anatomical, and psychiatric differences between men's and women's brains, those differences have not been scientifically connected to behavior (see http://brainrules. net/gender). So we must be careful not to use this rule as a confirmation of stereotypes but rather as an invitation to appreciate and value differences.

- Learn how genders differ in dealing with traumatic situations, styles of verbal communication, cementing relationships, and negotiating status.
- Work on understanding the role of emotions in teaching/learning.
- Use gender specific groups on occasion.
- Use teams of both genders to benefit from different perspectives, ways of processing information, and emotions.

Rule #12: We are powerful and natural explorers.

If we learn best by exploring and testing our world, then ample classroom "space" must be devoted to active exploration of our inner and outer worlds.

- Encourage and nurture the natural curiosity of learners. Appreciate questions.
- Incorporate into the learning environment exposure to real-world applications and to people who operate in the real world.
- Encourage learning about our brains and how they function.
- Cultivate and nurture a sense of childlike wonder about daily life.

Every leader owes it to his or her learners to create the best possible environment for learning. The best learning takes place when learners feel safe, nurtured, and empowered and have access to a rich repertoire of manageable and varied activities.

The Size of Your Group

The number of incoming leaders will determine the shape of many of the suggested activities. Small groups, an important part of this model, work best with at least four to six people. Larger groups can be subdivided effectively. Here are some ideas for adapting this model for various size groups.

Three or fewer leaders

- Consider a partnership with another congregation in your area. Different contexts can add depth and challenge to leaders' learnings. Leaders can share the leadership responsibilities.

- Lead the group yourself. This can be a great experience of getting to know the new leaders. You will be the process guide. Resist the temptation to be the content expert and allow the leaders to do and learn from their own work.
- Invite the whole (or part of the) session to participate in the workshops. Experienced leaders can be mentors to others. Session members can lead parts or all of a workshop. Everyone should participate in the group discussions and projects. You will have to remind current leaders not to deprive incoming leaders of the opportunity to learn and grow by doing their work for them.

Four to eight leaders

- Use pairs and triads or two groups of four.

Nine and more leaders

- Use groups of three or more persons.

Good to know . . .

- Smaller groups process assignments quickly.
- Have groups as even in size as possible.
- Move individual groups away from each other in the room (or have separate rooms) to reduce "eavesdropping" and loss of focus.
- Have an extra assignment ready to give groups that finish before others.

The Learning Space

The kind of space your group will need will depend, of course, on how many leaders are participating in the program. Here are some issues to consider:

- Use a space that will be relatively undisturbed throughout each class session.
- Ideally, everything except the faith-sharing groups will meet in the same space.
- Use a space large enough to accommodate discussions with the whole class and also suitable for those times when learners will be working in small groups around a table.
- If possible, set up for dinner and eat your meal in your meeting space. This makes the transition time to and from the meal (only thirty minutes) as short as possible.

- Provide tables as a place for reference materials and a writing surface.
- If possible, use an open square so everyone can see one another. A chevron pattern is also workable. Avoid straight rows of tables where many are facing other's backs.
- Provide name tents or nametags for participants.
- Have available extra pencils or pens and some writing paper for those who might need them.
- Any time a group of adults meets for this length of time, it is a good idea to provide beverages (at least water) and, if desired, a selection of snacks in the meeting room. Learners can then help themselves as needed.

Leader Preparation

Leaders will need to prepare for the workshops along with the learners. We are assuming that leaders of this model will be either pastors or educators with a background in the polity and theology of the Presbyterian /Reformed tradition. We provide the framework for the model, supply lesson outlines, worksheets, handouts, and a bibliography of resources. You will choose and develop the specific content and activities for each learning segment out of your own wisdom and style. We provide the building materials. You are the project manager.

Additionally, since there are many important areas of theology and polity that will not be covered in this workshop model, you may want to think about a two-, or even three-year cycle of theology and polity topics. Leaders can use the overall model for the leader development program and develop additional topics to meet the needs of a particular setting.

Handling Questions

If your experience is like ours, throughout the course, learners will have lots of questions, some clarifying the assigned materials plus many others on topics triggered by the discussions and assignments.

It is the leader's responsibility to balance the need for an immediate response to questions with the goal of working through the content as designed. Sometimes you will need to defer a question until a later time; sometimes you will need to throw out the lesson plan and capitalize on a more important interest. Only you can know which is appropriate. Here are some suggestions for handling the inevitable questions:

Accept the Questions

- Accept each question as a gift. Remember it takes courage to ask a question.
- Find something in the question to affirm. Dig deep if necessary.
- Connect the question with previous content and discussion.

Collect the Questions

- Provide a supply of 3x5 index cards. Invite learners to write down questions as they occur and turn in the card at the end of each class session.
- Post flipchart paper on the wall for learners to write down questions.
- Have a supply of stick notes handy. Learners write questions and post them on the black/whiteboard or on a flipchart.

Answer the Questions

- Carve five minutes out of each class session to respond to selected questions from the class. Be disciplined!
- Write your responses to selected questions in a FAQ (frequently asked questions) format and either distribute each week or compile for the end of the workshops.
- Save some questions and pose one or two of them at each session/diaconate meeting, inviting more experienced leaders to respond. (Be gentle if they don't know the answers. Think of this as an opportunity for continuing education!)

Learner Preparation

It is conceivable that leaders-elect could participate in this program without preparing for each class, but everyone would suffer. For maximum benefit, each participant will have to spend a significant amount of time in preparation for each class. Prior to each class there are assigned readings in *Called to Serve,* the *Book of Order,* the *Book of Confessions,* as well as worksheets to complete and sections of questions to answer or review in the *Participant Workbook* Study Guide.

While each learner will work at his or her own pace, it is likely that two to three hours or more of preparation will be required for each class. This is quite a time commitment. Here are some suggestions for making this commitment more palatable:

- Prepare the whole congregation in advance of the leader nominations process by introducing this new model for leader development in newsletter articles, bulletin announcements, postings on bulletin boards, or announcements at worship services, session, and diaconate meetings.

- Use the nominating process. Let persons being asked to serve as church leaders know about the leader development program *before* he or she agrees to be nominated. While you probably won't be able to tell them dates for the workshops until you have your calendar setting meeting, you can advise them of the general shape of the program and inform them of the intensity of preparation. Then, if someone agrees to be nominated, he or she is also agreeing to the work needed to prepare for serving as a church leader.
- Share your vision of how leaders who have been through this program will benefit the church. Talk about the importance of spiritually mature and knowledgeable leadership. In order to meet the challenges and needs of the church in the twenty-first century, reinforce the idea that the church will rise no higher than the level of its elected leaders.

Assignments in Advance

In order to make the best use of the limited class time, each learner will need to get all the assignments for the four workshops before the workshops begin. (See the Overview and Assignments Chart in appendix 1; it is also in the *Participant Workbook*.)

Each participant will need their own copy of the *Participant Workbook* (or *Workbook*). It will have all the basic resources to participate in the leader development course. You may, from time to time, need to provide other resources for your setting.

At some point, as you introduce this program, you may want to explain that a variety of teaching activities will be used in these workshops. Every workshop unit will ordinarily include

- Individual readings done prior to class
- Worksheets completed prior to class
- Small group discussion of the worksheets in table groups
- Mini-lectures or presentations by the leader(s)
- Class discussions of the content
- Faith sharing groups with the same groups meeting across all workshop units

While this model covers a lot of ground in short periods of time, it has been our experience that, with the fast pace, varied activities, and an emphasis on personal spiritual growth as well as learning content, most learners will be invigorated by the process and, instead of becoming bored, will wish there were more time together.

Required Resources for Learners

While you could let incoming leaders purchase their own copies of needed texts, we recommend the church order the books in advance and offer them to the incoming leaders as a package at cost. Having the leaders purchase their books gives them an investment in their learning. Your church may want to offer individual subsidies as needed. Each learner will need the following:

- A Bible: You may want to talk about the merits of various translations and paraphrases of Scripture, but all Scripture passages used here (unless otherwise noted) are from the New Revised Standard Version (NRSV).
- *Book of Confessions.* Louisville, KY: Office of the General Assembly, 2016.
- *Book of Order, 2019–2023.* Louisville, KY: Office of the General Assembly, 2019.
- *Making Disciples, Making Leaders—Participant Workbook,* 2nd ed., newly updated. Louisville, KY: Westminster John Knox Press, 2022.
- *Selected to Serve: A Guide for Church Leaders*, 2nd ed., newly updated. Louisville, KY: Westminster John Knox Press, 2022.

Denominational resources are available from the Presbyterian Store (www .pcusastore.com). Online versions are available from the denomination's website as free downloads for those who would like them in digital form. Check with your presbytery office each summer for any discounts that might be available as a result of bulk purchases through the presbytery.

NOTE: If the PC(USA) Constitution changes in the coming years, you should use the most recent editions of denominational resources and make the appropriate changes to references used in this *Leader's Guide* and the *Participant Workbook.*

Chapter 5

Bring Them to the Tent of Meeting

When Moses could no longer do the work alone, he cried out to God and God directed him to "bring them to the tent of meeting and have them take their place with you there; and I will take some of the spirit that is on you and put it on them; and they shall bear the burden of · the people along with you so that you will not bear it all by yourself."
(Num. 11:16b–17)

Why?

Worship shapes our identity as Christians. It defines who we are and our understanding of who God is. It establishes our frame of reference. In worship, leaders confess sin, reflect on the Scriptures, pray, and partake of Holy Communion. For the past thirteen years, both our session and diaconate have begun monthly meetings with worship. We go to "the tent of meeting," the place of worship. It has changed the way we meet.

It's difficult to bite at someone in a meeting when you just fed them the body and blood of Christ! When we worship together, we tend to be more compassionate in the way we address our differences. In worship we take on some of the nature and character of God. That nature spills over into the meeting and business of the church.

In the beginning, we had some who felt a half-hour of worship was too long, and we should get on with the business. We held our ground. Worship *is* our business. We added worship to the leader development classes. Every class begins with worship in the sanctuary. When they go to their first monthly meeting, worship seems the norm.

We've gone so far as to say to the leaders, "If you have to miss some part of the meeting, miss the business, but don't miss the worship." This sends the message that leadership in the church goes far beyond running an organization. Leaders need to be fed. Leaders need to pray for the congregation. Leaders need to study the Scriptures and receive the sacrament. The tent of meeting is a place where the Spirit shows up and empowers people for ministry.

Where?

We go to the *sanctuary*. In our case, we all sit in the chancel (the choir loft). In other churches, we have gathered chairs on the floor around the Communion table. Use whatever space you have, but don't sit in the pews. It's too formal, too structured, and it hinders a sense of community. (Maybe we should take the pews out for Sundays too!)

There's something about going to that sacred space that is different from having a brief devotional in your meeting room. It's intentional, it takes an effort, and it sets the tone.

What?

Every congregation is different. Worship in your way. This is what we do:

Call to Worship
Hymn/Song (Yes, we sing!)
Prayer of Confession / Assurance of Pardon
Scripture
Reflection / Discussion of the Text
Prayers
Communion (by intinction)
The Peace

In appendix 6, you will find the opening worship orders for each workshop session, plus worship suggestions for subsequent session and diaconate meetings throughout the church year. You will also find a list of Scriptures related to leadership to use in your monthly worship experiences (see appendix 7).

Worship needs to be thirty minutes. You can't afford to let it run over. Be a good steward of the time and keep things moving. The following is an overview of how we have a powerful worship experience within one thirty-minute time frame.

Our *call to worship* is simply, "The Lord be with you." We sing a *hymn*. (Hard to do with a small group, but possible.) We *confess* our sins and receive *pardon,* then we read Scripture related to the challenges and opportunities of leadership.

Rather than preach or provide a lecture, we open the floor for *discussion* on the text. "What does this say to us as leaders of the church? Does anything jump out or confuse you?" The team is discovering the truths of the text. That's empowering.

As the group enters into *prayer*, we invite individuals to speak a prayer concern and then have the group respond, "Lord, hear our prayer." Again, let them do the praying. A significant part of a leader's work is to pray for the congregation and for the world. This isn't a waste of time—it's their ministry.

We celebrate *Communion*. Have a loaf and cup and pass them around. They feed one another the body and blood of Christ. "The body of Christ broken for you. The blood of Christ shed for you." Very powerful! We don't use a lot of liturgy—just the Words of Institution.

Communion is followed by "the peace of Christ be with you" and the *sharing of the peace* with one another. This group is now ready to sit down together and consider the work of the church. This is the cultivation you are providing as the teaching elder. This is the "tent of meeting," the place of empowerment for ministry.

Who?

It was God's idea to have Moses gather the leaders at the tent of meeting, the place of worship. That sends a powerful message. "Let's start by getting straight who is who!"

Notice what God did *not* do. God did not have the leaders gather in a classroom or in a board room. This wasn't about knowledge, it was about empowerment. Could that be what has been missing in our churches for so many years?

The leaders were sent to the tent of meeting. If they don't go there, how can they lead others there? You can't give others something you don't have yourself.

As leaders, we need to worship. We need to pull away from the tasks of ministry and reattach to the One who calls us to ministry. It's a Mary and Martha thing. Sometimes you have to get out of the kitchen!

God didn't gather the leaders in the kitchen or in a committee or even in the mission field. God gathered the leaders at the tent of meeting. Don't let this one get by you. We are the ones who need to go there, first and foremost.

This may be the most transformational piece in our model of leadership development.

We Didn't See This Coming!

Several years ago, we used the session worship time to have a Service of Wholeness (see *Book of Common Worship*). It was one of the most powerful experiences any of us had ever had.

We formed three small circles, with ruling elders and a pastor in each (one circle works for smaller groups). We invited members of the congregation to come into the circle and ask for prayer for themselves or for someone else in need. The pastor then offered a prayer and anointed the person's forehead with oil, saying, "We anoint you in the name of the Father, the Son, and the Holy Spirit. Amen."

There were tears in every group. These are regular Presbyterians in a large church in a big city! We are a congregation of conservatives, moderates, and liberals. Everybody was into this, or perhaps this was into everybody.

When all was said and done, we sat in silence for some time. No one dared to speak. It was a holy moment.

From that experience, we decided to offer this service for our congregation regularly. We held it on a scheduled session night. The Service of Wholeness was the business of the session that night. That was it.

We publicized the service and made every attempt to explain what it was and what it was not. We had no idea if anyone would come. They did. It was not a huge crowd, but it didn't need to be. The ones who were there needed to be there, and here were their ruling elders praying for them and anointing them with oil. This is *way* past merely running a church!

So powerful was this service that the session decided to offer one every six months on a regularly scheduled session meeting night. The word got out, and every service has been well supported. Only recently have we decided to move the service off the regularly scheduled meeting, because now all of the ruling elders want to be a part of this service, this ministry for the congregation and community. Awesome.

Our Service of Wholeness (see appendix 6) was born out of the session having worship together at the start of every meeting. Leadership in the church must be empowered by the Holy Spirit and cultivated by us. We didn't see this coming!

Chapter Six

Design Your Course

What you are about to see is our model. It has evolved. We start with a Saturday, half-day retreat. That time is used for the "nuts and bolts" of coming on board as a deacon or ruling elder. We have some ice-breakers, go over the budget, hand out church policies, review the meeting schedules, provide organizational charts, bring them up to speed on current issues, expose them to online resources for the training, have some Q&A, and negotiate the meeting times for training.

We then set up four, three-hour-and-fifteen-minute workshops. We schedule them based on when the students can attend. So the classes are not every Wednesday or every Sunday. The goal is 100 percent attendance! We also spread the sessions out far enough so the students can complete the reading assignments.

Including preparation time, we estimate that students spend approximately thirty hours in our training program. *Stephen Ministry* requires forty hours plus prep time. DISCIPLE *Bible Study* requires eighty-five hours plus prep time. We're not out of line in expecting a commitment.

We highly recommend our model to you. It has been well tested. The results are positive. The quality of our leadership team has strengthened over the years. It does take time for it to become part of the church's culture.

Options

We're aware that not everyone can start with such an elaborate model of training. You have to decide what works best for you in your situation. There are other options.

Option # 1:   Use our materials for a retreat, Friday evening through Saturday. This option does not allow time to digest the material or to build the team.

Option #2:   Do a retreat and follow it with two or three workshop sessions (i.e., one a month). This allows time for the reading and for team building.

Option #3:   Use our materials to teach during the Church school hour. If you choose this option, we recommend at least a semester (with a retreat) or ideally two semesters (September–May).

If you use the entire school year, the nominees would be examined and installed before the course was completed. That's the downside. The upside is an extended amount of time to cover the material and to get to know one another. Sunday mornings are also convenient. This option does require a significant commitment from the clergy, who would be both preaching and teaching every Sunday throughout the semester or school year.

Option #4:   This is the model you will build. Something is better than nothing. Start somewhere, and the rest will evolve. What would be fun and rewarding for your group? Start there!

Other Considerations

Our model includes worship, two teaching units, a meal, and small, faith-sharing groups. Other options will sacrifice one or more of those experiences. We highly suggest you find a way to establish and maintain the small groups. This has received the highest rating in our model.

In sharing their personal faith, the ruling elders and deacons bond in a way not available in teaching units or even worship. They get to know and trust one another in their small groups.

So, if you choose another option, explore how you can set up the small, faith-sharing groups to go along with your choice. They could meet in homes once a month. We provide the worksheets for their discussions. Be creative!

The worship component would be the other sacrifice if you choose other options. What does worship have to do with training? The answer is *formation*.

Worship shapes the identity of leaders. We sing, confess, reflect upon Scripture, pray, and celebrate Communion together. If you choose another option, consider if there is a way to incorporate worship into your model. It would fit well into a retreat. We hope you can find ways to build worship into your training. We have found it to be instrumental in our shift from information to formation.

Solo pastors may feel you don't have time to do all of this. You probably don't. You could see this as just one more thing you have to add to an already full plate. No arguments here. So something would have to go in order for you to have the time to do this. Are there things you could hand off in order to make this investment? Are there "lesser things" that could give way to "greater things?" Only you can answer these questions. This leadership development would have to be something you want to do, or it will not happen.

What's in it for you? A stronger group of leaders in your church who could know some of the things you know and care about the things you care about. It could empower and unleash a team for ministry! It could add years to your ministry . . . and to your life.

Chapter 7

The Orientation Meeting

As soon as possible after the congregational election, get your leaders together for an initial meeting. There are two primary goals and several secondary goals, depending on your circumstances. The two primary goals can be covered in a one-hour meeting. Other goals may require an additional hour or more.

The primary goals of this meeting are to distribute the required books (and collect the money) and to negotiate the dates and times of the four workshops. You may find other ways to get the books to the leaders, but everyone should have them by this meeting.

The crucial task is negotiating workshop dates and times. The reason not to arbitrarily pick the dates and times in advance is the difficulty of getting 100 percent participation. Asking for 100 percent participation at all workshops lets the leaders know the importance of this process for the church. It also challenges them to make space in their personal lives for their development and growth as church leaders.

You can just ask leaders to bring their calendars to the meeting. But without some preplanning, the process is cumbersome. We have found using an online scheduling tool very helpful in narrowing down the possibilities. The scheduling tool at www.doodle.com works very well. You can specify the timeframe on multiple days at multiple times, send an email to your leaders, and the respondents mark the options that work for them. Doodle compiles the responses in a spreadsheet format, highlighting the selections that work best for the most people. If you dig a little into the settings when you are laying out your options, you'll find a yes/no/maybe choice that can provide more flexibility in choosing your dates.

Once you have the compiled results, you will have a good start at finding four or five dates/times that could work. Once leaders see and hear the commitment of others in the room—changing their schedules to make this a priority—they are more willing to adjust their own schedules.

Inevitably there will be unavoidable conflicts. Our practice is to allow leaders, if absolutely necessary, to miss only one workshop. They still have to do the assignments and are responsible for connecting with their group or leader to be accountable for the assignments and to review the workshop content. You may arrange to record any presentation for those who have to miss.

Once days and times are set, have the leaders record them on the Overview and Assignments Chart in their workbooks. A follow-up email or letter to confirm the dates/times will eliminate any ambiguity.

It would also be wise to review the Overview and Assignments Chart (see below) to make sure the leaders understand what's assigned and what's expected of them prior to the first workshop. Remember, in this model, most of the individual work is done outside of the workshops. Everyone is expected to have completed the assignments prior to attending the workshop.

If your church has a more complicated organization or has expectations that are not included in the model, then you may choose to extend the orientation session to allow more time to address your needs. After many years of having only four workshops, we added one more—to combine the orientation meeting with several other pressing needs. We chose a Saturday morning, shortly after the congregational election, to meet for about three-and-a-half to four hours. On our agenda was:

- A continental breakfast (food facilitates meeting) (30 min.)
- Distribution of books (during breakfast)
- Opening Worship / Devotion (15 min.)
- Vision for and Challenges of Leadership (30 min.)
- Nuts and bolts of Leadership (30 min.) [ruling elders and deacons meet separately]
- State of the Church (30 min.)
- Update on current challenges, prior decisions, financial stewardship expectations
- Workshop Scheduling / Overview (45 min.)

In our setting, we use an online course component that requires account setup and basic instructions for using the website and mobile app access. So we add an additional segment to our initial meeting. You may have special needs as well that could be added to this opportunity to have all the incoming leaders together. The four workshops are tightly packed, and it is difficult to add content to them. The orientation meeting is the chance to supplement the normal content of this model.

Leader Development Overview and Assignments

"The session shall provide a period of study and preparation, after which the session shall examine them as to their personal faith; knowledge of the doctrine, government, and discipline contained in the Constitution of the church; and the duties of the ministry. The session shall also confer with them as to their willingness to undertake the ministry appropriate to the order." (G-2.0402)

Workshop 3h:15m	Worship 30 min.	Part 1 45 min.	Meal 30 min.	Part 2 45 min.	Small Groups 45 min.	Assignments (To be done prior to the class.)
#1	Worship 1	**Personal Faith** Your Faith Journey and Call to Serve (a) Constitutional Questions a–i (overview) [see W-4.0404 a–i]				☐ Book of Order: preface ☐ Book of Confessions: preface, part iii, pp. xx–xxix ☐ Selected to Serve: Chapters 1, 7 ☐ Participant Workbook (PW): Study Guide Section 1 (1.1–1.6) ☐ Worksheet: My Fears and Concerns ☐ Worksheet: My Faith Journey ☐ Worksheet: Constitutional Questions
#2	Worship 2	**Doctrine and Theology** What Presbyterians Believe (c) The Bible and Essential Tenets (b, d)				☐ Book of Order: F-1, 2 ☐ Book of Confessions: prefaces to each confession ☐ Selected to Serve: Chapter 6 ☐ PW: Study Guide Section 2 (2.1–2.15) ☐ Worksheet: To Be or Not to Be—Reformed! ☐ Worksheet: Book of Confessions chart ☐ Worksheet: To Be a Christian
#3	Worship 3	**Governance, Worship, and Discipline** The Presbyterian Way (e, f, g, h) When Things Go Wrong (e)				☐ Book of Order: F-3; G-1, 2.01–0105, 3, 6; W-1, 2, 5; D-1, 2 ☐ Book of Confessions: Confession of 1967 ☐ Selected to Serve: Chapters 3, 4, 5, 8 ☐ PW: Study Guide Sections 3, 4, 5 ☐ Worksheet: Presbyterian Principles ☐ Worksheet: Worship True/False Quiz ☐ Worksheet: Case Study #1: Maintaining the Purity of the Church
#4	Worship 4	**The Work of Ministry** What Ruling Elders/Deacons Do (i) How This Church Works				☐ Book of Order: G-2.01–2.04 ☐ Book of Confessions: A Brief Statement of Faith ☐ Selected to Serve: Chapter 9 ☐ PW: Study Guide Section 6 (6.1–6.9); review questions 3.5, 3.6 ☐ Worksheet: Duties of Ordered Ministries ☐ Worksheet: Writing Your Statement of Faith ☐ Worksheet: (opt.) Writing Your Financial Stewardship Journey

Chapter 8

Workshop 1—Personal Faith

Your Faith Journey and Call to Serve (W-4.0404 a)

Do you trust in Jesus Christ your Savior, acknowledge him Lord of all and Head of the Church, and through him believe in one God, Father, Son, and Holy Spirit?

Constitutional Questions (W-4.0404 a-i)

The first workshop introduces the basic format for the subsequent workshops. It focuses on the leaders-elect's personal faith and call to serve and reviews the constitutional questions (W-4.0404 a-i).

Leaders-elect will have one primary group that will be their faith-sharing small group. Assign leaders to groups in advance, aiming for diversity in age, gender, experience in the church, and ruling elders and deacons. To provide some variety, you may let leaders form their own table groups for part 1 of the workshop. In any event, use the assigned groups for the small-group sharing at the end. The small groups remain the same for all four workshops.

Participant Assignments

Prior to this workshop participants will need to complete these assignments:

1. *Book of Order*: Read the preface
2. *Book of Confessions*: Read the preface, part iii, pages xx–xxix
3. *Selected to Serve:* Chapters 1, 7
4. *Participant Workbook*: Study Guide Section 1 (1.1–1.6)
5. Worksheet: My Fears and Concerns
6. Worksheet: My Faith Journey
7. Worksheet: Constitutional Questions

8. Review the "Prayer of Examen" exercise (*Participant Workbook*, Supplemental Resources, p. 57) which will be used in the workshop.

Outline of Workshop 1

Worship (30 min.)
- Use Opening Worship for Workshop 1, found at the end of this *Leader Guide* and in the *Participant Workbook*, or one of your choosing.

Part 1 (45 min.)
- "Constitutional Questions" worksheet: sharing/discussion in groups, large group discussion

Meal (30 min.)

Announcements/Housekeeping

Part 2 (30–45 min.)
- Faith stories of pastor(s) or current ruling elders

Small Groups (45–60 min.)
- In groups of 4–6, share faith stories ("My Faith Journey" worksheet)
- "Prayer of Examen" closing exercise (10–15 min.)

Commentary on Workshop 1

Worship

This first worship will set the tone, not only for subsequent worship services, but for the whole leader development process. Starting with worship establishes the importance of spiritual nurture and leadership over learning constitutional content (as important as that is).

See chapter 5, "Bring Them to the Tent of Meeting," for a suggested way to do worship.

Consider printing participant nametags that folks can collect along with the worship sheets when they arrive. This is also a convenient way to track attendance.

For each of the worship services, arrange for an accompanist to play the hymn and during Communion (or be prepared for someone to lead singing a cappella).

If possible, collect the responses to the "My Fears and Concerns" worksheet in advance. You may want to consider retyping the responses to mask authorship. Put the responses on individual sheets of paper. When participants arrive, have them pick one at random to read at the time of confession. Alternatively, collect the worksheets as participants arrive (cross off or tape over any names) and redistribute them randomly to the worshipers.

Start worship on time. Waiting until everyone arrives rewards those who come late and disrespects those who arrive on time.

Prepare the prayer of confession by inviting worshipers to read the responses to "My Fears and Concerns." Suggest a brief pause for reflection between each response.

Consider dividing the group into different voices to read a portion of the Scripture readings. For example, in the Numbers 11 passage, you could have a narrator, Moses, and the LORD as separate voices.

The meditation on the text is a group reflection on what the text says in its original context and further reflection on what the text has to say about leadership in God's church today. Some possible questions for this passage might be:

- What made the LORD angry?
- How did Moses respond?
- What was Moses's solution?
- How did God respond?
- What was God's solution?
- What is the leadership takeaway in this passage?

Part 1—Constitutional Questions

Form small groups of 4–6. They will use the "Constitutional Questions" worksheet, following the instructions on the second page. Allow about thirty minutes for the groups to deal with their own questions and then call everyone back together. Invite the sharing of questions that arose in the small groups and offer your wisdom.

Meal

Invite someone to offer a blessing for the meal. If participants will be paying for their meal, arrange for someone to collect money.

Announcements/Housekeeping

As you reconvene the group, make any brief announcements or clarifications needed. You may want to highlight the date and assignments for the next workshop.

Part 2—Faith Sharing

This first sharing exercise sets the tone for openness and straight talk about personal faith. How the workshop leaders share their own faith journeys will model the kind of sharing the leaders-elect will copy.

The first exercise asks workshop leaders to share their own faith journeys. It is helpful to have two people share their journeys, to highlight the different paths we all take on our journeys. Two ten-minute stories followed by questions from the group will easily fill a thirty-minute timeframe. If there is only a single pastor, invite a wise ruling elder to share her or his journey. As you prepare to give and tell your faith story, resist the temptation to write or present a novel—think short story!

Once the leaders have shared their stories, the leaders-elect may do so. Separate the participants into their preassigned groups. It is best for each group to have their own space so as not to be distracted by other groups. Send the groups off to share their faith stories using the "My Faith Journey" worksheet. Remind the groups they are responsible for their time and to save 10 minutes at the end for the closing exercise.

Give some instruction as to how you would like the group to end in a time of prayer. We have used the "Prayer of Examen" exercise found in the *Workbook*. This ancient spiritual exercise (from St. Ignatius of Loyola, 1491–1556) provides a structure for prayer at the end of the day. It may help those who don't ordinarily pray with others. Some may find its form too restrictive. Find a pattern that works for your groups and encourage a time of mutual prayer to close out the workshop. Whatever the form, closing with a unison Lord's Prayer is appropriate.

Teaching Alternatives

The structure and activities listed above reflect our experience of what works in approaching this material. It will work for some settings and not for others. We encourage you find the particular structure and activities that work for you. To prompt your creativity, here are some alternative ideas:

Part 1

- For smaller groups stay together and share responses to the worksheet.
- Instead of the worksheet, use the discussion questions at the end of each section in *Selected to Serve*, chapter 7, "The Ordination Vows."
- Develop your own resources

Part 2

- Study some of the call stories in the Scriptures (e.g., Abraham, Moses, Samuel, Paul) to note similarities and learnings for our call to serve.
- Video record other clergy and previous leaders telling their call stories. Make the videos available for viewing outside class (e.g., YouTube, Vimeo).

Chapter 9

Workshop 2—Doctrine and Theology

What Presbyterians Believe (W-4.0404 c)

Do you sincerely receive and adopt the essential tenets of the Reformed faith as expressed in the confessions of our church as authentic and reliable expositions of what Scripture leads us to believe and do, and will you be instructed and led by those confessions as you lead the people of God?

The Bible and Essential Tenets (W-4.0404 b, d)

Will you fulfill your ministry in obedience to Jesus Christ, under the authority of Scripture, and be continually guided by our confessions?

Participant Assignments

1. *Book of Order*: F-1, 2
2. *Book of Confessions*: prefaces to each confession
3. *Selected to Serve*: Chapter 6
4. *Participant Workbook*: Study Guide Section 2 (2.1–2.15)
5. Worksheet: To Be or Not to Be—Reformed!
6. Worksheet: *Book of Confessions* chart
7. Worksheet: To Be a Christian

Outline of Workshop 2

Worship (30 min.)
- Use Opening Worship for Workshop 2 or another order of your choosing

44

Part 1 (45 min.)—What Presbyterians Believe
- "To Be or Not to Be—Reformed!" worksheet
- Sharing/discussion in groups, large group discussion
- "Some Essential Tenets of the Reformed Faith" handout (see *Workbook* "Supplemental Resources," p. 46. Copy and distribute to participants)

Meal (30 min.)

Announcements/Housekeeping

Part 2 (45 min.)—Confessions
- Confessions group activity
- Large group discussion

Small Group Activity (45 min.)
- "To Be a Christian" worksheet sharing
- Closing prayers

Commentary on Workshop 2

Worship

Follow pattern from Workshop 1, or provide your own order of worship.

Part 1—To Be or Not to Be—Reformed!

In small groups, have participants share their responses to the "To Be or Not to Be—Reformed!" worksheet. Invite them to share the reasons for their responses (about fifteen minutes). Once everyone has responded, ask the group to attempt a consensus, which they will note in the column marked G (Group) (about ten minutes). Call the groups back into a large group and offer your responses to the statements, making the case for why a particular statement is or is not consistent with the Reformed tradition. You may want to review and study the statements in advance and prepare your responses. Some statements can be argued in multiple ways.

At the end of this time, distribute the handout on "Some Essential Tenets of the Reformed Faith," which is a summary of the Presbyterian/Reformed framework, taken from the *Book of Order,* F-2.0300–2.0500.

Part 2—Confessions Group Activity

You will need to prepare for this activity in advance. In *Leader Guide* appendix 2, find the *"Book of Confessions*: Worksheet Answer Key." Print each entry in the chart on a separate placard or card (index card, letter, legal, or tabloid size). For each confession, you will have four placards—name, location, date, themes. Make one set of placards for every 7–8 participants. Keep each set of placards together, but shuffle them so they are no longer in order. Spread out the placards on the floor in the classroom or hallway, and invite the group(s) to put them in order without using any notes. This is a group exercise, and participants should share their memory and knowledge with one another to get the group's chart as accurate as possible. If there is more than one group, after twenty minutes or so, invite the groups to review each other's charts for accuracy. Then allow participants to get their notes and *Book of Confessions* to check their work.

Reconvene the large group, and address any questions that have arisen. You may also want to give a mini-lecture on why we have multiple confessions and what role the confessions have in our church.

Small Group Activity—To Be a Christian Worksheet

Send the group(s) off to share their responses to the worksheet. Remind them to allow ten minutes at the end for sharing prayer concerns (possibly using the "Prayer of Examen") and ending with the Lord's Prayer.

Teaching Alternatives

Instead of focusing on the ordination vows, focus on the Bible and biblical interpretation.

- Assign the worksheet "The Bible Tells Me So" (*Participant Workbook*, "Alternate Worksheets," p. 69).
  - At the workshop, invite participants to position themselves in the room on a virtual scale (one wall is strongly agree, the opposite wall is strongly disagree).
  - Once positioned, invite participants to share their reason(s) for their position with someone nearby. Share your own position when asked.
- Distribute the handout "The Bible in Our Confessions" (*Participant Workbook*, "Supplemental Resources," p. 51), and review the development of our view of the Bible over the centuries.

- Distribute the handout "Guidelines for Understanding and Use of Holy Scripture" (*Participant Workbook*, "Supplemental Resources," p. 47), which summarizes "The Presbyterian Understanding and Use of Scripture."

Focus on where the Church finds its authority.

- Assign the worksheet "Authority in the Church" (*Participant Workbook*, "Alternate Worksheets," p. 59).
  - See *Book of Order*, F-1, 2, 3, for the Presbyterian perspective.
  - Have participants share their rankings and discuss.
  - Consider this order: Jesus Christ, Bible, Essential Tenets, Testimony and Experience of the Church, Private Understanding, and Personal Experience.
  - Share your understanding of where the Church finds its authority.

Prepare a lecture and/or slide presentation reviewing the eleven confessions, highlighting key content. Have participants interact with the material in some way, such as the following:

- Recite the Apostle's Creed together.
  - What questions arise from this creed?
- Read the Brief Statement of Faith (or sections) together.
  - How is this creed similar/different from the Apostle's Creed? What questions does it raise?

Chapter 10

Workshop 3—Governance, Worship, and Discipline

The Presbyterian Way (W-4.0404 e, f, g, h)

Will you be governed by our church's polity, and will you abide by its discipline? Will you be a friend among your colleagues in ministry, working with them, subject to the ordering of God's Word and Spirit?

Will you in your own life seek to follow the Lord Jesus Christ, love your neighbors, and work for the reconciliation of the world?

Do you promise to further the peace, unity, and purity of the church?

Will you pray for and seek to serve the people with energy, intelligence, imagination, and love?

When Things Go Wrong (W-4.0404 e)

Will you be governed by our church's polity, and will you abide by its discipline? Will you be a friend among your colleagues in ministry, working with them, subject to the ordering of God's Word and Spirit?

Participant Assignments

1. *Book of Order*: F-3; G-1, 2.01–.0105, 3, 6; W-1, 2, 5; D-1, 2
2. *Book of Confessions*: Confession of 1967
3. *Selected to Serve*: Chapters 3, 4, 5, 8
4. *Participant Workbook*, Study Guide Sections 3, 4, 5
5. Worksheet: Presbyterian Principles
6. Worksheet: Case Study: Maintaining the Purity of the Church

Outline of Workshop 3

Worship (30 min.)
- Use Opening Worship for Workshop 3, or another of your choosing.

Part 1 (45 min.)—The Presbyterian Way
- "Presbyterian Principles" worksheet
- Exchange responses / small group(s)
- Large group discussion / clarification of principles

Meal (30 min.)

Announcements/Housekeeping

Part (45) Worship / Discipline
- (30 min.) "Worship True/False Quiz" worksheet
- Exchange responses in small group(s)
- Large group review of key principles from quiz
- (15 min.)—Present a mini-lecture on "When Things Go Wrong: a Brief Overview of Discipline in the PC(USA)"

Small Group Activity (20–25 min.)
- Small group discussion of case study: "Maintaining the Purity of the Church"

Large Group Discussion (20–25 min.)
- See case study for questions
- "Life Together in the Community of Faith: Standards of Ethical Conduct for Ordained Leaders in the Presbyterian Church (U.S.A.)"
- Prayer concerns
- Closing prayer (in large group)

Commentary on Workshop 3

Worship

Follow the pattern of Opening Worship for Workshop 3, or provide your own order of worship.

Part 1—The Presbyterian Way

Most folks are aware that Presbyterians are different from other denominations but can't say exactly how. This segment helps clarify some of the unique ways that Presbyterians see themselves and do their work. The assigned worksheet, "Presbyterian Principles," is designed to get folks deeper into the principles than just writing an outline from the *Book of Order*. Many of the principles listed in our Constitution are presented in archaic language that will require struggle to bring them into today's world. The small group sharing allows participants to hear others' interpretation of what these principles mean. After twenty to thirty minutes, call everyone back together and see what questions have arisen. You won't have time to cover all the principles, so choose ahead of time the three or four you want to emphasize, especially if they don't come up in the discussion.

Part 2—Worship and Discipline

Invite your small group(s) to exchange responses to the "Worship True/False Quiz." Gather folks together and work through selected statements. Give the correct answers (see appendix 2, "Worship True/False Quiz: Answer Key," pp. 79–80) and encourage participants to question what is unclear. Focus on three to five key principles for further explanation.

Since discipline in the church is the most unknown part of our practice as Presbyterians, we suggest you prepare a short (fifteen minute?) mini-lecture on the purpose, role, and basic elements of discipline in our church. In addition to basic philosophy and terminology, share some examples from your own experience as you have seen discipline applied in the church.

Small Group(s)—Maintaining Purity, Ethical Conduct

The recommended format for this segment is different than normal. After a brief introduction, it combines processing the case study, "Maintaining the Purity of the Church," with the small group sharing and large group discussion. That is, the small groups do not go off by themselves but stay with the whole class.

Use half of your time to discuss the case in small groups. Put participants in their small groups (in your primary meeting room) and, depending on the size of your groups, give them twenty to twenty-five minutes to process the case study. If you suspect some people have not read the case study you may want to review it along with the discussion questions. The small groups should first make sure each member is clear on the details of the case and then take each discussion question in turn, hearing from each member before moving to the next question. When you sense the groups have finished, direct everyone's attention back to you in the large group.

Use the remaining time to discuss the case in the large group, look at ethical guidelines for church leaders, and have your closing prayer. You may want to test the sense of the group by asking them to stand in the room between opposite walls (strongly agree > strongly disagree) to indicate their response to the statement: Joan should tell someone what she knows. Then ask them to explain why they are standing where they are standing.

Then work through each of the discussion questions in turn.

Call attention to "Life Together in the Community of Faith: Standards of Ethical Conduct for Ordained Leaders in the Presbyterian Church (U.S.A.)" (p. 54 in the *Workbook*). Highlight the guidelines you think have the most bearing on this case study. Encourage the leaders-elect to review the guidelines in more detail in the coming days.

Finally, conclude with a time of prayer using the "Prayer of Examen" or another form of your choosing. At least invite participants to offer prayer concerns and end by saying the Lord's Prayer together.

Teaching Alternatives Parts 1 and 2

If you have several groups, instead of assigning the "Presbyterian Principles" worksheet, assign each group to one or more sections of the Constitution and ask them to develop a four- to six-minute (maximum) presentation on their assigned area.

Group 1—Governance: G-1, 2.01–2.0105, Congregations and Ordered Ministry
Group 2—Governance: G-3, 6, Councils and Amending the Constitution
Group 3—Worship: W-1, 2, Dynamics and Elements of Worship
Group 4—Discipline: D-1, 2, Principles of Discipline and Judicial Process

Each group should include an overview of the area and its key ideas and concepts, focus on what a new leader needs to know, use any method or means to present content and engage learners, and help learners understand the importance and significance of the material. "Invisible points" are gained for creative and imaginative presentations.

Provide time and space for the presentations and mention any important principles not covered by the presentations.

Another approach is to use downloadable resources available (at minimal cost) from the PCUSA Store (www.pcusastore.com). You may want to assign *The Basics of Presbyterian Polity* and *The Basics of Reformed Worship* to read and discuss. Both are from the Leader Reader series available at minimal cost from the PCUSA Store (www.pcusastore.com).

Consider using resources from www.theocademy.com. In the *Preparation for Ordered Ministry* series you will find "Lesson Eight: Principles of Order and Government," "Lesson Ten: The Dynamics of Worship," "Lesson Eleven: The Word in Worship," "Lesson Twelve: The Sacraments in Worship," and "Lesson Thirteen: Prayer and Song in Worship," all of which have downloadable study guides. Choose one or more, show the videos in class, and use them as a discussion starter for how Presbyterians govern and do worship.

Small Group(s)—Maintaining the Purity of the Church

- Invite a leader from your presbytery (presbytery executive, member of the Committee on Ministry, etc.) to talk about church discipline, especially times when discipline has been restorative.
- Invite a Presbyterian lawyer to compare and contrast the US legal system with the Presbyterian system of church discipline.
- Create a simulation of a hypothetical disciplinary hearing dealing with an issue between congregations. Pre-assign roles and provide content to create a "live" case study. Have participants act out their roles for a brief time and then debrief the experience.
- Use one of the other case studies provided in the *Participant Workbook*.

Chapter 11

Workshop 4—The Work of Ministry

What Ruling Elders / Deacons Do (W-4.0404 i)

(1) (For ruling elder) Will you be a faithful ruling elder, watching over the people, providing for their worship, nurture, and service? Will you share in government and discipline, serving in councils of the church, and in your ministry will you try to show the love and justice of Jesus Christ?

(2) (For deacon) Will you be a faithful deacon, teaching charity, urging concern, and directing the people's help to the friendless and those in need, and in your ministry will you try to show the love and justice of Jesus Christ?

(3) (For teaching elder) Will you be a faithful teaching elder, proclaiming the good news in Word and Sacrament, teaching faith and caring for people? Will you be active in government and discipline, serving in the councils of the church; and in your ministry will you try to show the love and justice of Jesus Christ?

(4) (For ruling elder commissioned to particular pastoral service) Will you be a faithful ruling elder in this commission, serving the people by proclaiming the good news, teaching faith and caring for the people, and in your ministry will you try to show the love and justice of Jesus Christ?

Participant Assignments

1. *Book of Order*: G-2.01–2.04
2. *Book of Confessions*: A Brief Statement of Faith
3. *Selected to Serve*: Chapter 9

    4. *Participant Workbook*: Study Guide Section 6 (6.1–6.9); review questions
      3.5, 3.6
    5. Worksheet: Duties of Ordered Ministries
    6. Worksheet: Writing your Statement of Faith
    7. Worksheet: (optional) Writing your Stewardship Faith Journey

Outline of Workshop 4

Worship (30 min.)
- Use Opening Worship for Workshop 4, or one of your choosing.

Part 1 (45 min.)—Duties of Ordered Ministry
- "Duties of Ordered Ministry" worksheet
- Sharing/discussion in groups, large group discussion, Q&A

Meal (30 min.)

Announcements/Housekeeping

Part 2 (45 min.)—How This Church Works
- Presentation on organizational structure of congregation (e.g. organizational chart)
- Presentations on specific duties of ruling elders and deacons in your congregation
- May include pastor, clerk of session, moderator of Board of Deacons

Small Groups (45 min.)
- In small groups have each participant share the draft of their faith statement (35 min.)

Prayer of Examen Closing Exercise (10 min.)

Commentary on Workshop 4

Part 1—Duties of Ordered Ministry

Focus on the duties of ordered ministry as explained in the *Book of Order* and any duties and responsibilities particular to your congregation.

    Divide into groups of 4–6 (not the faith-sharing groups) and have participants share their responses to the assigned worksheet: "Duties of Ordered

Ministries." Encourage groups to collaborate and come to group consensus. After some time, call the groups back into the large group and respond to any questions arising from the group discussions.

If your church has trustees, clarify their role and responsibility as compared to that of ruling elders and deacons.

Consider highlighting that teaching elders are members of the session.

Part 2—How Your Church Works

The focus here is the organizational structure of your church and any responsibilities of ordered ministries specific to your congregation. It may also include information on how to get things done (the proper way to "run with an idea"), who in the church to go to for specific issues, and how the financial stewardship of the church is managed (e.g., how to request a payment, read the financial statements, etc.).

You may want to invite key leaders to make presentations. This is a great time to showcase the leadership of your congregation.

Let the incoming leaders know of any unique traditions or expectations for those in ordered ministries (serving Communion, making hospital visits, teaching, making financial stewardship calls, etc.).

You may want to provide participants with:

- An organizational chart of church governing bodies and committees
- Committee and ministry team descriptions
- A sample financial statement
- Your vision/mission statement
- Your church by-laws
- A list of who to contact for what with e-mail and phone numbers
- Other documents specific to your setting

Small Groups—Sharing Personal Faith Statements

When the small groups assemble, they are to listen to each person share her or his personal statement of faith. The small group should provide feedback and encouragement and offer observations about anything that is not clear. This experience is the initial run through for the faith statement that will be presented at the session exam.

When everyone is finished sharing, the group should conclude their time by sharing prayer concerns and having a time of prayer (e.g., "Prayer of Examen," Lord's Prayer) to close.

Teaching Alternatives

Part 1

- Consider using the video "Lesson One: Ordered Ministry" from the *Preparation for Ordered Ministry* series at www.theocademy.com as a supplement for this section.
- Assign one or more sections of the downloadable resource from www.pcusastore.com, such as *Serving as Elder, Serving as Deacon, Serving as Trustee,* and discuss in class.

Part 2

- Do a walkthrough of your financial statement, highlighting how money is turned into ministry.
- Create a hypothetical case of a member who has brought a "great idea" to a ruling elder or deacon. Explore the best way to work that idea through your system.

Looking Ahead

Either at your housekeeping time or subsequent to Workshop 4, inform your leaders of what happens next regarding

- The session examination (see recommendations in the next chapter)
- The ordination/installation service
  - Date, time, logistics
- An evaluation of the leader development experience
  - See *Workbook* "Post-Class Evaluation," p. 40.

Post-Class Evaluation

At the end of your leader development period, we suggest you poll the group for feedback. You will discover areas of weakness and strength among the activities. Comments and suggestions from the participants will help improve your process and content each year.

The following evaluation is based on the pre-class survey and collects feedback on all aspects of this model. Keeping the pre- and post-class surveys similar will help you assess growth the leaders experienced through their participation in the development process.

We use a Constant Contact e-mail survey (www.constantcontact.com). Survey Monkey (www.surveymonkey.com) is also a good online tool for gathering feedback. You may want to develop a printed evaluation to distribute.

Create your own means to get feedback, but ask incoming leaders for help in improving the leader-development experience. You will receive insightful and useful suggestions.

Chapter 12

Session Examination

Once you have completed the leader development workshops, you'll need to set the date for the session examination of the ruling elders and deacons-elect. The process we suggest can be done as part of a regular session meeting or as a separate meeting for just the examination. The exam (see G-2.0402) may be done by the whole session or, if necessary, a commission of the session (see G-3.0109b (1)).

We have found that a one-on-one examination can be intimidating for all involved. Our suggestion is to have two or three ruling elders examine a group of two or three leaders-elect. One of the currently serving ruling elders will be designated the "table moderator" and will be responsible for managing that group's examination.

If it is difficult to secure enough ruling elders to have two or three per group of leaders-elect, it works well to recruit ruling elders not in active service to assist in the examination. Often, ruling elders report that being involved in the examination process is a high point for them, whether or not they are currently serving on the session. They also express appreciation for being reminded of the things that make us Presbyterian as they hear responses from the leaders-elect.

If you use ruling elders not in active service, make sure you have the proper numbers of ruling elders for the examination to be official: in the case of using the whole session, a quorum is required; in the case of the commission, the minimum number of ruling elders and clergy is required.

We recommend having a meal together before the examination. The meal serves several purposes. Presbyterians are always pleased to gather around a table. In this informal fellowship setting, previous and current ruling elders can get to know the leaders-elect over table conversations. The mealtime provides a time buffer so that folks who may be running late do not interrupt an examination already in progress. Enjoying a meal together also helps to reduce (though not completely) the anxiety many leaders-elect experience prior to the examination. You may want to consider making the leaders-elect guests for the meal (at the church's expense) as a way of saying thanks for all the hard work of preparation and their willingness to serve the congregation as a ruling elder or deacon.

Preparation for the Exam

Prior to the time of the examination, there are a number of things to do.

- Set the date and time of the exam very early in the process (even before the nominating committee develops a slate of nominees) so that everyone can schedule it on their calendars.
- You may want to schedule a make-up date to handle the inevitable schedule conflicts. This is a great opportunity to use a session commission for examining a smaller number of people.
- Make arrangements for the meal, if there is to be one.
- Based on the number of leaders-elect to be examined, recruit the needed number of table moderators and other ruling elders to conduct the exam.
- Provide reminders to all involved regarding date, time, location, cost of meal, expectations, and any other logistical issues.
- Provide examining ruling elders a copy of the Study Guide with answers (see *Leader Guide* appendix 3, p. 83).
- Note: it is often the case that ruling elders, in preparing for the examination, reinforce their own knowledge of the areas covered in the exam—a significant plus for everyone.
- Give some thought to assigning seating groups for both the current ruling elders and the leaders-elect. It is wise to provide a mix of male-female, seasoned-novice, introvert-extrovert elders at each table.

The Faith Statement

Each leader-elect, as part of their preparation for the examination, will develop a statement of faith to be read and shared as the first part of their examination. The faith statement is one concrete way for ruling elders to know something of the personal faith of each leader-elect.

We ask each person being examined to bring two copies of their faith statement (prepared in the workshops) with them to the examination—one to turn in and one to keep for their files. The faith statements are kept on file with the pastor(s) and are not otherwise distributed.

Since faith statements are personal and subjective by nature, there is no right or wrong to be evaluated. Each faith statement needs to be accepted as a gift from the leader-elect. Nevertheless, at the time of the examination, table moderators and examining elders may determine that a particular faith statement is deficient if it is obvious that little thought went into it or that it is clearly the telling of a faith journey (biography and history) rather than a statement of what the person believes. In such situations, it may be appropriate to ask the leader-elect to rewrite the statement. Review of the faith statement by the group in Workshop 4 should make this unnecessary.

The Examination Step by Step

If you are having a meal (recommended), allow thirty to forty-five minutes for eating and time for fellowship around the table.

At the appointed time for the exam, convene the session or commission with prayer and any instructions that might be necessary. It's always helpful to remind all involved of the sequence of events and what's expected. Remind all that the table moderators will guide the process. If you are using the suggested grouping (two or three ruling elders with two or three leaders-elect) the examination will take about forty-five minutes.

The first task is for the leaders-elect to share their statements of faith. This is not a time for debate or discussion but a time to receive with appreciation this expression of personal faith. Questions for clarification or requests for elaboration are appropriate.

The table moderator may additionally choose some or all of the questions in section one of the Study Guide dealing with personal faith. It is appropriate to ask each question of each leader-elect in turn. Once all leaders-elect at the table have shared their statements of faith and responded to other questions in the area of personal faith, move to the next phase of the exam.

At this point the table moderator will become the guide through the examination in the proscribed content areas: knowledge of the doctrine, government, and discipline contained in the Constitution of the church; and the duties of the office. (G-2.0402)

The Study Guide is divided into sections based on these content areas. The table moderator will generally introduce a new content area with a question chosen from that section. Other ruling elders at the table my also pose questions from the Study Guide. It will be the table moderator's job to watch the clock and keep the process moving to conclude within the time allowed.

The leaders-elect are permitted to bring their copy of the Study Guide and the answers they have made to the questions with them to the examination. In one sense this is an "open book" examination. The examinees may refer to their notes, as there is no expectation of having memorized all the information. However, the leaders-elect are expected to be familiar enough with the material to use their own words and not read verbatim from their notes.

The Study Guide is just that—a guide for examiners and examinees. Ruling elders conducting the examination may come up with their own questions but are encouraged to avoid esoteric areas where even die-hard Presbyterians fear to tread.

Questions should be addressed to specific leaders-elect with the encouragement for other leaders-elect to add their additional comments or responses. Table moderators will need to ensure that one knowledgeable or gregarious leader-elect doesn't monopolize the answer time to the exclusion of the other examinees.

Five minutes or so before the end of the allotted time, someone can provide an appropriate five-minute warning so table moderators can wrap up the examination.

When time is up, give everyone a break. During this time, meet with the table moderators to determine if there are any concerns regarding any leader-elect being adequately prepared to serve in ordered ministry.

While it may seem the "Christian" thing to do is to approve *everyone's* examination, this is the time to guarantee the integrity of the process of preparation for service. When might it be appropriate to question the readiness of a leader-elect to serve? While there will be variation in each individual examination, every leader-elect is expected to prepare, at least minimally, for the examination. If it is clear that a person simply did not bother to prepare, perhaps trusting that he or she would not be held accountable for a lack of preparation, this is the time to question his or her readiness to serve. The high expectations of this model of church leader development will be difficult to maintain in the future if word gets out that it doesn't matter whether or not you prepare.

There also may be situations in which it becomes apparent that a leader-elect cannot affirm some "essential tenet" (e.g., does not believe in infant baptism, or denies the sovereignty of God, etc.) or is unable to answer all ordination questions affirmatively.

In these cases, it is appropriate to suspend for a time the examination of the individuals in question and not take action on their examination at this session meeting. While certainly awkward, doing so gives some needed time for members of the session (or perhaps its commission) to confer privately with the leaders-elect to raise concerns and determine appropriate actions. This also provides public witness to the session's intention to maintain the integrity of the preparation and examination process.

The possibility of such an event taking place (however unlikely) suggests that the examination date be scheduled several days or weeks in advance of the service during which ruling elders and deacons are to be ordained (where needed) and installed, to provide adequate time to address any concerns.

After the table moderators have conferred, and the session (or commission) is reconvened, a motion to approve the examination of the leaders-elect is in order. Having voted in the affirmative, the ruling elders and deacons can be welcomed. If the examination is done by a commission of the session, their work concludes as normal. If the examination is a part of a session meeting, the session may invite the leaders-elect to stay for the remainder of the meeting.

Following the model established in the worship segments of the leader development workshops, it is suggested that a brief worship and Communion service be included as part of the examination. Depending on your pattern for such things, worship and Communion could take place immediately following the vote approving the examination or it could be scheduled as the last item on the session agenda before adjournment. In either case, celebrating the Lord's Supper together can be a powerful witness to the grace that will support your common ministry in the years to come. Some groups find that participating in Communion while standing in a circle further reinforces the sense of shared ministry.

Chapter 13

"When a Horse Dies, It's an Excellent Time to Dismount!"

*O*nce the training is over, the new leaders join an already existing team. You wouldn't want to invest all that time and energy in training and then bring them onto a dysfunctional or ineffective team. You have to work on both sides of the equation.

Someone once said, "When a horse dies, it's an excellent time to dismount!" No one in their right mind would keep trying to ride a dead horse, but we do it in the church. We are prone to hold on to things that worked once but are no longer effective. With shrinking memberships and budgets, we can no longer afford to be complacent. Some things do need to be preserved. Other things need to be changed. Leaders in the church today need to know the difference.

Identify Your "Dead Horses"

Is there anything dead about your deacon or session meetings? There is a way to find out.

Ask each group to identify the "Top 10 Dead Horses in Our Church." Have them share their lists and create a composite list, noting which "dead horses" received more than one vote. Then ask them to prioritize the list. "What are our top three? Would we be willing to discontinue anything on the list?" You may agree to remove several of the less controversial ones first. Removing "dead horses" frees time, money, and energy to create new avenues of ministry.

Our Top Three Dead Horses

When we took inventory, we discovered our top three "dead horses" were:

1. meeting too long
2. micromanaging
3. listening to reports

Can a session or diaconate meeting have life in it? We think so. Years ago, we moved away from the listening-to-reports model. Our session meetings now have an "Order of the Day," a single focus for the meeting. This allows us time to get our heads and hearts around something significant in the life of the church.

It is crucial that each committee or council submit a brief report to the session with an update of their work and action items needed (use bullet points, not minutes). You may have to coach them in the beginning as to what constitutes an "action item." Does the session really need to vote on this? In some cases they do, just for the buy-in and authority. You'll find, however, that many things can be entrusted to the committees to decide and take action. We always give the session an opportunity to pull anything off of the reports for discussion, clarification, or reconsideration. The session is always in charge. No end runarounds. Build the trust.

We researched the *Book of Order* to determine what a session actually has to vote on, and we discovered only six items:

1. Electing ruling elders to serve as commissioners to presbytery and electing the clerk and treasurer.
2. Approving the budget.
3. Membership matters (receive, transfers, deletions, etc.).
4. Calling congregational meetings.
5. Approving examinations of ruling elders and deacons.
6. Worship matters (baptisms, The Lord's Supper, etc.).

Everything else can be delegated and supervised. The session can empower committees, councils, and task forces to accomplish the work of ministry within the budget and boundaries of that work.

This *empowerment* must be coupled with *accountability*, which requires a healthy amount of *trust*. Sessions that see themselves as "Rule Keepers" and need to micromanage will not do well with this model. Rule keepers will scrutinize all committee work and in many cases redo it.

When a session empowers its committees to do their work, it frees the session meetings from routine reports and voting on routine matters. Session meetings can focus on the 30,000-feet issues. Imagine how stimulating such meetings are for leaders. It allows them to get outside of the box, expand their vision, and even dream.

When we first moved to the Order-of-the-Day format, we invited our various ministry areas to take a month to be with the session. The schedule looked like this:

January—Missions/Outreach
February—Education/Faith formation
March—Worship
April—Leader Examinations
May—Strategic Visioning Team
June—Pastoral Care
July—No Meeting
August—Stewardship
September—Children's Ministry
October—Youth Ministry
November—Budget
December—A Social Event

By having one Order of the Day, the session can get a firm grasp of the strengths and challenges within each ministry area. It is also a wonderful experience to invite each ministry area to join the session for the opening worship and Communion. They experience the ruling elders studying Scripture, praying, having Communion, and in fellowship together. Powerful.

As time went by, we began to bring in a variety of Orders of the Day. One meeting was devoted to discussing recent General Assembly actions. As mentioned earlier, we held several Services of Wholeness each year on a session night. We've had meetings dedicated to capital campaign planning, endowment and major gifts, creating a new worship service, and starting a local mission project.

The point is, by moving away from micromanaging, the session has time to embrace the significant issues within the church. The meetings are more focused and give leaders an opportunity to lead.

Our session meetings begin with a meal (5:30–6:30 pm), followed by worship (6:30–7:30 pm), and a meeting with an Order of the Day (7:00–8:30 pm). Because we are shifting focus and rooms, the time goes by quickly. The meetings are energizing, spiritually uplifting, and an excellent use of a leader's time. We removed our top three "dead horses" and replaced them with more efficient ways of being together.

Our diaconate, or Board of Deacons, is committed solely to pastoral care. They are organized into various teams to accomplish their ministry. Deacon meetings also begin with worship, and they use their meetings as ongoing training sessions in pastoral care. One meeting may be dedicated to

"Listening" and another to "Grief." Each meeting fuels the deacons for this work of ministry.

First Steps

Anytime you are planning to make some changes, it is wise to form a session-approved task force to lay out the plans. Get buy-in and sketch out a timeline. Set a start date for the new and improved meeting model and then suggest trying it for one year. At that time you can evaluate its effectiveness, make some adjustments, and move ahead. Ownership is key. Never put an apple on your head by demanding these changes or springing it without notice. Make it a team effort and the results will be long-lasting.

Chapter 14

Other Opportunities
for Leadership Development

Create a College of Ruling Elders

There is no such thing as a "College of Ruling Elders" in the *Book of Order*, but a number of PC(USA) churches have them. Every ruling elder of the church, whether or not in active service, is a member of the College of Ruling Elders. Every other year we have a College of Ruling Elders Banquet. Spouses are included. We also invite anyone who has served as a ruling elder in another PC(USA) church. What we discovered was that they enjoyed being together. It's like "old home week." Our senior ruling elders really appreciate being included. The saying, "Once an elder, always an elder" comes to life!

We charge for the event and cater a really nice meal. A team decorates the tables, and musicians play during dinner. We honor our oldest and youngest ruling elders. We recognize those who have served in other churches. We read the names of those who have died since our last gathering. It is an evening of celebration and thanks.

A signup list is placed on each table. Opportunities are given to help serve Communion, participate in baptisms, deliver homebound Communion, and several other ministry needs. The lists come back full of names. People want to be included. This is the core of your church.

We began sending the monthly session minutes to the College of Ruling Elders. Again, they expressed deep appreciation for being kept in the loop. "You haven't forgotten me," we heard from many of them. They also become effective spokespersons within the congregation in interpreting and supporting session actions and decisions.

We hold our banquet in January on a Friday evening prior to a Saturday Leadership Retreat. We have invited speakers on a variety of topics. We kicked off a major capital campaign at a College of Ruling Elders Banquet.

It's a great time to rally the troops and invest something into your leadership. It pays high dividends!

Form an "Emerging Leaders" Group

What are "Emerging Leaders"? We saw a need to cultivate the thirty–forty-year-old group within our church. Some churches have very few members in this age group. You can start with whatever you have. The idea is to be proactive in cultivating new leadership within the church.

We compiled a list of names and invited them to an "Emerging Leaders Discipleship Challenge." A light meal was followed by a forty-five-minute program. Childcare was provided. That's key. The program has to be good. The appeal is for them to deepen their discipleship and to become leaders in the church. There are lots of ways to creatively get that message across.

We held a "Discipleship Challenge" every quarter for the first year. They were well attended. We had a few outside speakers, used some funny videos, had table conversations, and gave door prizes.

At the end of the first year, we invited them to join a "Supper Club." Small groups were formed that met in homes. They determined their own schedules. We provided Bible study materials. Leaders were born!

Do Something Different

Leaders need to be cultivated, nurtured, challenged, and supported. This takes intentional, long-term commitment. Just stop to consider what a church is without healthy leadership at the helm. It drifts. It panics. It complains. It argues. It is visionless. It sits on "dead horses." It fails. It may even die.

So, on a scale of 1 to 10, how important do you think all this leadership cultivation is? On a scale of 1 to 10, how would you rank your efforts at equipping the leadership of your church? Compare the two. Do your efforts match the importance you ascribe to it? (Now we're down to the altar call!)

So what do you do next? Take some of our suggestions and try something. Start small. Form a task force and plan for change. Put together a new system. Sell the need to your session. Get their ownership and participation. Launch something new.

Conclusion

"*I*f you always do what you've always done, you'll always get what you've always gotten." That can be a good thing, or it can mean it's time to change. What is the end result you want?

It's an oxymoron when a pastor laments working alone and feeling isolated but does little or no training, equipping, motivating, or empowering of the lay leadership within the church. It's called *reaping what you sow*.

Having said that, what we are proposing is not easy. There will be resistance. You may be criticized for demanding too much. That's why we recommend presenting this new model to your session for approval. They need to own it. Don't put the apple on your head!

You could start with a session-appointed taskforce to explore the options for improving your training process. You could custom design your own model using our resources. Get the buy-in and call your first training class a *pilot group*. Ask for their feedback to tweak your model for the next group. We tweak our model every year!

The more critical issue is that of raising the bar. You get what you ask for—usually. If you don't ask for much, that's what you get. We discovered that our deacons and ruling elders want this to be a life-changing experience. They want to grow in their faith. They don't want to merely run a church. Take them to higher ground.

As pastor, there's something in here for you too. Your role as *teaching* elder is intensified in our model. You will discover true partners in ministry. You could soon feel as though you are working on a team. When you are enjoying what you are doing, it no longer feels like work.

Our invitation is for you to simply try this. Commit to just one year. See if it fits your style. Make it your own. Ask for feedback. If you see positive results, adjust the model and try it again the next year. After a three-year cycle, everyone on the diaconate and session will have been trained under the new model. That's when you should see the most significant difference.

Appendix 1

Leader Nominating Form and Leader Development Overview and Assignments

Leader Recommendations

Class of _____

Pick out from among you . . . [those] . . . of good repute, full of the Spirit, and of wisdom, whom we may appoint to this duty. Acts 6:3

We are currently seeking servant leaders to serve a three-year term as ruling elders and deacons of our church. Your recommendations, with comments, would be appreciated. To qualify, candidates must be a member for at least one year, a faithful participant in worship and the life of the church, and a financial steward who faithfully contributes to its ministry.

Leader Nominating Committee

DEADLINE FOR RECOMMENDATIONS: SUNDAY _____

Desired Personal Qualities*

Deacons	**Elders**
Deacons should be persons of spiritual character, honest repute, of exemplary lives, brother and sisterly love, sincere compassion, and sound judgment. *(from the Book of Order, G-6.0401)*	Elders should be persons of faith, dedication, and good judgment. Their manner of life should be a demonstration of the Christian gospel, both within the church and in the world. *(from the Book of Order, G-6.0303)*

*Please note that one does not need to serve as a deacon before becoming a ruling elder.

How to Recommend a Leader:

Submit to _____ at the church office or by:

Website: _____

Mail: _____

_____

E-Mail: _____

Leader Recommendation Form

❏ for Ruling Elder   ❏ for Deacon
❏ Youth Ruling Elder ❏ Youth Deacon

In order to submit a candidate, it is required that you provide the candidate's name *and* your name in case we have questions. Please elaborate on personal qualities, involvement in our church, and why you consider him/her to be a good candidate for church leadership.

Candidate's name:_____

Comments: _____

_____

_____

_____

_____

_____

_____

_____

_____

_____

_____

Ruling elders serve in one of the following ministry areas: Administration, Adult Education, Children and Family Ministries, Congregational Life, Outreach, Stewardship, Worship, or Youth Ministries. If you are recommending a candidate for ruling elder, in which ministry area would this individual best serve?

_____

_____

Your name: _____

Date: _____

Phone: _____

Leader Development Overview and Assignments

"The session shall provide a period of study and preparation, after which the session shall examine them as to their personal faith; knowledge of the doctrine, government, and discipline contained in the Constitution of the church; and the duties of the ministry. The session shall also confer with them as to their willingness to undertake the ministry appropriate to the order." (G-2.0402)

Workshop 3h:15m	Worship 30 min.	Part 1 45 min.	Meal 30 min.	Part 2 45 min.	Small Groups 45 min.	Assignments (To be done prior to the class.)
#1	Worship 1			**Personal Faith** Your Faith Journey and Call to Serve (a) Constitutional Questions a–i (overview) [see W-4.0404 a–i]		☐ **Book of Order:** preface ☐ **Book of Confessions:** preface, part iii, pp. xx–xxix ☐ **Selected to Serve:** Chapters 1, 7 ☐ **Participant Workbook (PW):** Study Guide Section 1 (1.1–1.6) ☐ **Worksheet:** My Fears and Concerns ☐ **Worksheet:** My Faith Journey ☐ **Worksheet:** Constitutional Questions
#2	Worship 2			**Doctrine and Theology** What Presbyterians Believe (c) The Bible and Essential Tenets (b, d)		☐ **Book of Order:** F-1, 2 ☐ **Book of Confessions:** prefaces to each confession ☐ **Selected to Serve:** Chapter 6 ☐ **PW:** Study Guide Section 2 (2.1–2.15) ☐ **Worksheet:** To Be or Not to Be—Reformed! ☐ **Worksheet:** *Book of Confessions* chart ☐ **Worksheet:** To Be a Christian
#3	Worship 3			**Governance, Worship, and Discipline** The Presbyterian Way (e, f, g, h) When Things Go Wrong (e)		☐ **Book of Order:** F-3; G-1, 2.01–0105, 3, 6; W-1, 2, 5; D-1, 2 ☐ **Book of Confessions:** Confession of 1967 ☐ **Selected to Serve:** Chapters 3, 4, 5, 8 ☐ **PW:** Study Guide Sections 3, 4, 5 ☐ **Worksheet:** Presbyterian Principles ☐ **Worksheet:** Worship True/False Quiz ☐ **Worksheet:** Case Study #1: Maintaining the Purity of the Church
#4	Worship 4			**The Work of Ministry** What Ruling Elders/Deacons Do (i) How This Church Works		☐ **Book of Order:** G-2.01–2.04 ☐ **Book of Confessions:** A Brief Statement of Faith ☐ **Selected to Serve:** Chapter 9 ☐ **PW:** Study Guide Section 6 (6.1–6.9); review questions 3.5, 3.6 ☐ **Worksheet:** Duties of Ordered Ministries ☐ **Worksheet:** Writing Your Statement of Faith ☐ **Worksheet:** (opt.) Writing Your Financial Stewardship Journey

Appendix 2

Answer Keys to Participant Worksheets

Everything You Ever Wanted to Know about Ruling Elders and Deacons: Questionnaire Answer Key

Note: See the questionnaire without answers in the *Participant Workbook,* "Alternate Worksheets," p. 61.

True or False

1. Deacons and ruling elders serve under the mandate of the session.

   False: "Members and those in ordered ministries serve together under the mandate of Christ." (G-2.0101)

2. The ordered ministries (deacon/ruling elder) are gifts to the church to minister and care for the congregation in whatever needs it may have.

   False: "Ordered ministries are gifts to the church to order its life so that the ministry of the whole people of God may flourish." (G-1.0102)

3. The call to ordered ministry in the Church is the act of the Nominating Committee and congregation.

   False: "The call to ordered ministry in the Church is the act of the triune God." (G-2.0103)

4. Those being nominated to serve in ordered ministry should meet six basic qualifications.

   True: 1. gifts and abilities
   2. strong faith
   3. dedicated discipleship
   4. love of Jesus Christ as Savior and Lord
   5. Their manner of life should be a demonstration of the Christian gospel
   6. They must have the approval of God's people and the concurring judgment of a council of the church. (G-2.0104a)

5. Candidates for ruling elder/deacon should be examined on their knowledge of the Bible, the organization of their particular church, and their positions on certain social issues.

> **False**: "The examination shall include, but not be limited to, a determination of the candidate's ability and commitment to fulfill all requirements as expressed in the constitutional questions for ordination and installation (W-4.0404)." (G-2.0104b)

6. To be in ordered ministry in the church is to exercise freedom of conscience within certain bounds.

> **True**: "It is to be recognized however, that in entering the ordered ministries of the Presbyterian Church (U.S.A.), one chooses to exercise freedom of conscience within certain bounds." (G-2.0105)

7. The ministry of the deacons is to be determined by the session. Deacons perform all duties of the church that the ruling elders cannot or choose not to perform.

> **False**: "The ministry of deacon as set forth in Scripture is one of compassion, witness, and service, sharing in the redeeming love of Jesus Christ for the poor, the hungry, the sick, the lost, the friendless, the oppressed, those burdened by unjust policies or structures, or anyone in distress." (G-2.0201)

8. Ruling elders, together with teaching elders, exercise leadership, government, spiritual discernment, and discipline and have responsibilities for the life of a congregation as well as the whole church, including ecumenical relationships.

> **True**: (G-20301)

9. A Nominating Committee must consist of six members, three men, three women, one of which must be a ruling elder serving on the session, one a deacon currently serving, and the pastor.

> **False**: "Congregations may provide by their own rule for a congregational nominating committee, provided that the committee shall consist of at least three active members of the congregation, and shall include at least one ruling elder who is currently serving on the session. The pastor shall serve as ex-officio and without vote." (G-2.0401)

10. It is not necessary for all newly elected leaders to participate in a training program, but they must be approved by the session as qualified before the congregation elects them.

> **False:** "When persons have been elected to the ordered ministry of ruling elder or deacon, the session shall provide a period of study and preparation, after which the session shall examine them as to their personal faith; knowledge of the doctrine, government, and discipline contained in the Constitution of the church; and the duties of the ministry. The session shall also confer with them as to their willingness to undertake the ministry appropriate to the order." (G-20402)

11. The Nominating Committee must choose from persons who have been active members for at least one year.

> **False:** There is no such rule.

12. Neither a husband and wife, nor any two people from the same family, can serve on the session or diaconate at the same time.

> **False:** There is no such rule. Each congregation can approve its own rules and guidelines for the Nominating Committee, as long as those rules are in keeping with the *Book of Order.*

Book of Confessions: Worksheet Answer Key

Note: See the worksheet without answers in the *Participant Workbook*, "Workshop 2: Doctrine and Theology," p. 24.

Confession	Date(s)	Location	Historical Context / Issues / Themes
Nicene Creed	4th Century	Constantinople	Personhood of Jesus Christ Reality of Holy Spirit
Apostles' Creed	2nd-8th Century	Rome, North Africa, Gaul	One God in Three Persons God as Creator
Scots Confession	Mid-16th Century	Scotland	"Election" and the Church
Heidelberg Confession	Mid-16th Century	Germany	Stewardship and the Lord's Supper
Second Helvetic Confession	Mid-16th Century	Switzerland	Covenant and Baptism
Westminster Confession	Mid-17th Century	England	Sovereignty of God Authority and Interpretation of Scripture
Shorter Catechism	Mid-17th Century	England	What Christians Should Believe Duties of Christian Life
Larger Catechism	Mid-17th Century	England	Guidance for Preachers on Confession's Doctrines
Theological Declaration of Barmen	Early 20th Century	Germany	Sin of Idolatry Lordship of Christ
Confession of 1967	Mid 20th Century	USA	Reconciliation in Church and Society
Belhar Confession	Late 20th Century	South Africa	Racial Apartheid, Unity, Reconciliation, and Justice
Brief Statement of Faith	Late 20th Century	USA	Jesus Christ's Life and Ministry Human Equality

Worship True/False Quiz: Answer Key

See the quiz without answers in the *Participant Workbook*, Workshop 3: "Governance, Worship, and Discipline," p. 30.

True   1. There can be no worship without mission and outreach.*

True   2. Being in a particular structure, familiar or not, does not guarantee that people will be treated with Christian love or respect.**

True   3. As church leaders, we are especially responsible to the church in our prayer life.***

False   4. Presbyterians celebrate four sacraments: the Lord's Supper, baptism, weddings, and funerals. (W-3.0401)

True   5. The sacraments are the Word of God enacted and sealed in the life of the church, the body of Christ. (W-3.0401)

True   6. All children are eligible for baptism. (W-3.0403)

False   7. A child being baptized in a Presbyterian church must have parents who are members of a Presbyterian church. (W-3.0403)

True   8. No one can be excluded from the Lord's Table. (W-3.0409)

False   9. Children are not allowed to partake of the Lord's Supper until they are confirmed. (W-3.0409; W-4.0202)

True   10. Music, art, drama, movement, media, banners, vestments, furnishings, and architecture can become idolatrous in worship. (W-1.0204)

True   11. Those responsible for worship are to be guided by the reformed tradition, the tradition of the local congregation, and openness to diversity and inclusive language. (W-2.0101; W-1.0302)

True   12. In a particular church, the clergy are to provide for worship and shall encourage the people to participate fully and regularly in it. (W-2.0305)

False   13. The session has authority to choose Scriptures, lessons to be read, to oversee the prayers offered on behalf of the people, and to choose the music to be sung. (W-2.0305)

False 14. The sequence or proportion of the elements of worship are the responsibility of the session with the concurrence of the pastor. (W-2.0305)

False 15. The sermon is the heart of worship. (W-3.0301)

True   16. In worship, music is not to be for entertainment or artistic display. (W-1.0204)

True   17. The teaching elder has responsibility for the selection of the version of text from which the Scripture lessons are read in public worship. (W-2.0304)

True   18. The congregation may read Scripture responsively, antiphonally, or in unison as a part of the service. (W-3.0303)

True   19. Only a minister can invite another minister to preach in his or her pulpit. (W-2.0303)

False 20. It is possible to be re-baptized if someone has a conversion experience. (W-3.0402)

False 21. Baptism is authorized by the clergy and can be celebrated in private or public worship. (W-3.0403)

False 22. The session assumes responsibility for nurturing the baptized person in the Christian life. (W-4.0201)

True   23. It is appropriate to celebrate the Lord's Supper as often as each Lord's Day. (W-3.0409)

* Johnson, *Selected to Serve*, 55.
** Ibid., 61.
*** Ibid., 63.

Duties of Ordered Ministries: Worksheet Answer Key

Note: See the worksheet without answers in the *Participant Workbook*, "Workshop 4: The Work of Ministry," p. 36.

Duty	Teaching Elder	Ruling Elder	Deacon
1. Be responsible for the life of a congregation as well as the whole church, including ecumenical relationships.	G-2.0301	G.2-0301	
2. Equip the saints for the work of ministry (Eph. 4:12).	G-2.0501		
3. Exercise compassion, witness, and service.			G-2.0201
4. Exercise leadership, government, spiritual discernment, and discipline.	G-2.0301	G-2.0301	
5. Help those burdened by unjust policies or structures.			G-2.0201
6. Preach the faith of the church.	G-2.0501		
7. Serve as faithful members of the session.	G-3.0201	G-2.0301 G-3.0201	
8. Support the people in the disciplines of the faith amid the struggles of daily life.	G-2.0501		
9. Serve as preachers of the Word.	W-2.2007 W-3.3401		
10. Share in the redeeming love of Jesus Christ for the poor, the hungry, the sick, the lost, the friendless, the oppressed, or anyone in distress.			G-2.0201

(continued on the next page)

Duty	Teaching Elder	Ruling Elder	Deacon
11. Serve as presbyters participating in the responsibilities of governance, seeking always to discern the mind of Christ and to build up Christ's body through devotion, debate, and decision.	G-2.0501		
12. Administer font and table to interpret the mysteries of grace and lift the people's vision toward the hope of God's new creation.	G-2.0501		
13. Distribute the bread and wine at Communion.	W-2.0304	W-2.0304 W-3.3616(d)	G-2.0202 W-3.0414
14. Stand for election as commissioners to higher councils.	G-2.0301	G-2.0301	
15. Have particular responsibility for the exercise of pastoral care within the community of faith.	W-5.0204	W-5.0204	W-5.0204

Appendix 3

Study Guide for Exam: Answer Key

The session shall provide a period of study and preparation, after which the session shall examine them as to their personal faith; knowledge of the doctrine, government, and discipline contained in the Constitution of the church; and the duties of the ministry. The session shall also confer with them as to their willingness to undertake the ministry appropriate to the order. (G-2.0402)

See the Study Guide form in the *Participant Workbook*, "Preparation," p. 5. The leaders-elect will use these questions to prepare for the session exam. At that examination, table moderators will choose from among these questions in examining the incoming leaders. Leaders-elect will be able to take their completed document with them to the exam.

Leaders-elect can answer most of these questions by judicious use of the indices in the *Book of Order* and the *Book of Confessions*. They are encouraged to note constitutional references as they research the questions.

The answers provided here are meant to be a guide for the table moderators.

1. Personal Faith (no right or wrong answers)

1.1. What is the story (outline) of how you came to be a person of faith?
  • individual response—no right or wrong answer
1.2. What people have been influential in the development of your faith? In what ways?
  • individual response—no right or wrong answer
1.3. Over the course of your life, what are some of the things that have increased your faith? What has challenged your faith?
  • individual response—no right or wrong answer

1.4. What are some of the factors that went into your decision to accept the call to be a church leader?
- individual response—no right or wrong answer

1.5. Which constitutional question is the most challenging for you? (See W-4.0404.) Why?
- individual response—no right or wrong answer
- See the list of Constitutional Questions (W-4.0404) following this answer key, pp. 93–94.

1.6. [REQUIRED QUESTION] What, if any, of the ordination questions can you not, in good conscience, answer in the affirmative? Why?
- NOTE: If a candidate indicates there is a question he or she cannot answer in the affirmative, make note of the person and the question and report to the session moderator or session member responsible for the exam.

2. Knowledge of Doctrine

2.1. Who is the head of the Presbyterian Church (U.S.A.)?
- F-1.0201: "God has put all things under the Lordship of Jesus Christ and has made Christ Head of the Church, which is his body."

2.2. What does it mean to say "God alone is Lord of the conscience?"
- F-3.0101: God Is Lord of the Conscience
  - a. That "God alone is Lord of the conscience, and hath left it free from the doctrines and commandments of men which are in anything contrary to his Word, or beside it, in matters of faith or worship."
  - b. "Therefore we consider the rights of private judgment, in all matters that respect religion, as universal and unalienable: We do not even wish to see any religious constitution aided by the civil power, further than may be necessary for protection and security, and at the same time, be equal and common to all others."
  - In the end, we are responsible to God alone for our beliefs and actions. Neither councils nor their actions may bind us in ways that violate our integrity before God.

2.3. Which of the Great Ends of the Church has the highest priority for you? Why?
- Leaders-elect may choose from among those listed in F-1.0304: The Great Ends of the Church
  - the proclamation of the gospel for the salvation of humankind;
  - the shelter, nurture, and spiritual fellowship of the children of God;
  - the maintenance of divine worship;

− the preservation of the truth;

− the promotion of social righteousness; and

− the exhibition of the Kingdom of Heaven to the world.

2.4. What is a confession?

- *Book of Confessions*, Preface: "A confession of faith is an officially adopted statement that spells out a church's understanding of the meaning and implications of the one basic confession of the lordship of Christ."

2.5. Why are confessions important in our tradition?

- *Book of Confessions*, Preface, p. xiv states five uses to which the confessions have been put in our tradition:

  − **Worship**—confessions as acts of praise, thanksgiving, and commitment in the presence of God

  − **Defense of Orthodoxy**—preserving the authenticity and purity of the faith

  − **Instruction**—education of leaders and members of the church

  − **Rallying Point in Times of Danger and Persecution**—prepare and strengthen Christians in times of challenge

  − **Church Order and Discipline**—ministers and church officers are required to accept the teachings of the confessions in order to be ordained

2.6. Why do we have more than one confession?

- The Church acknowledges the dynamic nature of belief arising out of particular circumstances and contexts. We cannot, in any one moment of time, express a statement of faith for all of time.

- F-2.01: "The creeds and confessions of this church arose in response to particular circumstances within the history of God's people. They claim the truth of the gospel at those points where their authors perceived that truth to be at risk. They are the result of prayer, thought, and experience within a living tradition. They appeal to the universal truth of the gospel while expressing that truth within the social and cultural assumptions of their time. They affirm a common faith tradition, while also from time to time standing in tension with each other."

2.7. How many confessions are in the *Book of Confessions*?

- Eleven (11)

2.8. What is the purpose of the *Book of Confessions*?

- F-2.01: "In these statements, the church declares to its members and to the world who and what it is, what it believes, and what it resolves to do." . . . "These statements identify the church as a community of people known by its convictions as well as by its actions. They guide the church in its study and interpretation of the Scriptures; they summarize the essence of Reformed Christian tradition; they direct the church in maintaining sound doctrines; they equip the church for its work of proclamation. They serve to strengthen personal commitment and the life and witness of the community of believers."

2.9. Which two confessions are shared by all Christians worldwide (the Church catholic)?
   • The Apostles' Creed and the Nicene Creed

2.10. Which confessions were formed in the twentieth century, and what were their particular historical contexts?
   • The Theological Declaration of Barmen (1934)—the rise of Nazi Germany—focus on the Lordship of Jesus Christ
   • The Confession of 1967—the Civil Rights movement—focus on reconciliation.
   • The Brief Statement of Faith (1983)—after the reunion of the northern and southern Presbyterian churches.

2.11. What are some *watchwords* of the Protestant Reformation?
   • F-2.04: "In its confessions, the Presbyterian Church (U.S.A.) upholds the affirmations of the Protestant Reformation. The focus of these affirmations is *God's grace in Jesus Christ* as revealed in the Scriptures."
   • "The Protestant watchwords—*grace alone, faith alone, Scripture alone*—embody principles of understanding that continue to guide and motivate the people of God in the life of faith."

2.12. What is the *central affirmation* of the Reformed Tradition?
   • F-2.05: "Central to this tradition is the affirmation of the majesty, holiness, and providence of God who in Christ and by the power of the Spirit creates, sustains, rules, and redeems the world in the freedom of sovereign righteousness and love."

2.13. Name one other affirmation of the Reformed Tradition.
   • F-2.05: "Related to this central affirmation of God's sovereignty are other great themes of the Reformed tradition:
      – The election of the people of God for service as well as for salvation;
      – Covenant life marked by a disciplined concern for order in the church according to the Word of God;
      – A faithful stewardship that shuns ostentation and seeks proper use of the gifts of God's creation; and
      – The recognition of the human tendency to idolatry and tyranny, which calls the people of God to work for the transformation of society by seeking justice and living in obedience to the Word of God."

2.14. Name one element the church is called to as the body of Christ.
   • F-1.01: "In Christ, the Church participates in God's mission for the transformation of creation and humanity by
      – proclaiming to all people the good news of God's love,

⁻ offering to all people the grace of God at font and table, and

⁻ calling all people to discipleship in Christ.

- Human beings have no higher goal in life than to
  ⁻ glorify and enjoy God now and forever,
  ⁻ live in covenant fellowship with God, and
  ⁻ participate in God's mission."

2.15. Why does the Presbyterian Church (U.S.A.) have such a strong emphasis on diversity and inclusiveness?

- F-1.0403: "The unity of believers in Christ is reflected in the rich diversity of the Church's membership. In Christ, by the power of the Spirit, God unites persons through baptism regardless of race, ethnicity, age, sex, disability, geography, or theological conviction. There is therefore no place in the life of the Church for discrimination against any person."

3. Knowledge of Government

3.1. What documents make up the Constitution of the Presbyterian Church (U.S.A.)?

- F-3.04: The Constitution Defined—The Constitution of the Presbyterian Church (U.S.A.) consists of the *Book of Confessions* and the *Book of Order*.

3.2. What are the parts of the *Book of Order*, and what is each part's special focus?

- A change in the constitution has increased the parts from three to four. The most observant leaders-elect will have noted the discrepancy and should be able to give you all four as listed in F-3.04:
  ⁻ Foundations of Presbyterian Polity—the basic principles that guide us as Presbyterians
  ⁻ Form of Government—how we are organized to do our work
  ⁻ Directory for Worship—how we, both corporately and privately, offer our lives in worship
  ⁻ Rules of Discipline—how we are to deal with one another in times of dissension and conflict

3.3. Name one of the Principles of Presbyterian Government.

- See F-3.02 and foreword
  ⁻ The **particular churches** of the Presbyterian Church (U.S.A.) wherever they are, taken collectively, **constitute one church**;
  ⁻ This church shall be **governed by presbyters** (elders and ministers of the Word and Sacrament, traditionally called ruling and teaching elders);
  ⁻ These **presbyters shall come together in councils** (traditionally called judicatories or courts or councils) in regular gradation;

- **Presbyters** are not simply to reflect the will of the people, but rather **to seek together to find and represent the will of Christ**;
- **Decisions shall be reached in councils by vote**, following opportunity for discussion, and a majority shall govern;
- A higher **council shall have the right of review and control over a lower one** and shall have power to determine matters of controversy upon reference, complaint, or appeal;
- Presbyters (ruling elders and teaching elders) are ordained only by the authority of a council;
- **Ecclesiastical jurisdiction is a shared power**, to be exercised jointly by presbyters gathered in councils;
- Councils possess whatever administrative authority is necessary to give effect to duties and powers assigned by the Constitution of the church.

3.4. What are the three ordained ministries in the Presbyterian Church?
   - G-2.0102 Ordered Ministries: The Church's ordered ministries described in the New Testament and maintained by this church are **deacons** and **presbyters** (**teaching elders** and **ruling elders**).

3.5. What are the duties and responsibilities of ruling elders and sessions?
   - G-2.0301: **Ruling elders**, together with teaching elders, exercise leadership, government, spiritual discernment, and discipline, and have responsibilities for the life of a congregation as well as the whole church, including ecumenical relationships. When elected by the congregation, they shall serve faithfully as members of the session. When elected as commissioners to higher councils, ruling elders participate and vote with the same authority as teaching elders, and they are eligible for any office.
   - G-3.0201: The **session** shall have responsibility for governing the congregation and guiding its witness to the sovereign activity of God in the world, so that the congregation is and becomes a community of faith, hope, love, and witness. As it leads and guides the witness of the congregation, the session shall keep before it the marks of the Church (F-1.0302), the notes by which Presbyterian and Reformed congregations have identified themselves throughout history (F-1.0303), and the six Great Ends of the Church (F-1.0304).
   - In light of this charge, the session has the responsibility and power to:
     - Provide that the Word of the God may be truly preached and heard.
     - Provide that the sacraments be rightly administered and received.
     - Nurture the covenant community of disciples of Christ.

3.6. What are the duties and responsibilities of deacons and the Board of Deacons?
   - G-2.0202: Deacons may be individually commissioned or organized as a Board of Deacons. In either case, their ministry is under the

supervision and authority of the session. Deacons may also be given special assignments in the congregation, such as caring for members in need, handling educational tasks, cultivating liberality in giving, collecting and disbursing monies to specific persons or causes, or overseeing the buildings and property of the congregation. Deacons shall assume other duties as may be delegated to them by the session, including assisting with the Lord's Supper (W-3.3616).

3.7. Name the four councils in the Presbyterian system and briefly describe their function(s).
- G-3.0101: The Presbyterian Church (U.S.A.) is governed by councils composed of presbyters elected by the people (F-3.0202). These councils are called
  - the **Session**—which governs the particular, local congregation,
  - the **Presbytery**—which governs a regional group of congregations,
  - the **Synod**—which governs a group of presbyteries,
  - and the **General Assembly**—which governs all presbyteries as a denomination.

3.8. How do you understand this statement from the *Book of Order*: "Presbyters are not simply to reflect the will of the people, but rather to seek together to find and represent the will of Christ" (F-3.0204)?
- Commissioners to councils are not sent with instructions from their constituency nor are they to "represent" a constituency, but are expected to seek to discern God's will together in the midst of the council's deliberations.
- No council can "bind the conscience" of its commissioners, that is, compel them to vote in a certain way.

4. Knowledge of Worship and Sacraments

4.1. Name the six elements of Christian worship.
- W-2.1000—Prayer
- W-2.2000—Scripture Read and Proclaimed
- W-2.3000—Baptism
- W-2.4000—The Lord's Supper
- W-2.5000—Self-Offering
- W-2.6000—Relating to Each Other and the World

4.2. What is the typical order of service in Presbyterian worship?
- W-3.3202:
  - Gathering around the Word
  - Proclaiming the Word
  - Responding to the Word
  - The sealing of the Word (Sacraments)
  - Bearing and following the Word into the world

4.3. What part does Scripture play in our worship and life together?
- W-2.2001 Centrality of Scripture: The church confesses the Scriptures to be the Word of God written, witnessing to God's self-revelation. Where that Word is read and proclaimed, Jesus Christ the Living Word is present by the inward witness of the Holy Spirit. For this reason the reading, hearing, preaching, and confessing of the Word are central to Christian worship. The session shall ensure that in public worship the Scripture is read and proclaimed regularly in the common language(s) of the particular church.

4.4. What is the primary role of music and musicians in worship?
- W-2.1004 Music as Prayer: Choir and Instrumental Music: To lead the congregation in the singing of prayer is a primary role of the choir and other musicians. They also may pray on behalf of the congregation with introits, responses, and other musical forms. Instrumental music may be a form of prayer since words are not essential to prayer. In worship music is not to be for entertainment or artistic display. Care should be taken that it not be used merely as a cover for silence. Music as prayer is to be a worthy offering to God on behalf of the people (see also W-2.2008; W-3.3101).

4.5. Name the sacraments that are celebrated in the Presbyterian Church (U.S.A.).
- Two (2)
- W-1.3033(2): The Reformed tradition understands baptism and the Lord's Supper to be sacraments, instituted by God and commended by Christ.

4.6. What are the biblical roots of each of the sacraments?
- See also—annotations for W-2.3000 and 2.4000 in *Book of Order* for specific Scripture references.
- W-2.3001 Jesus and Baptism: Baptism is the sign and seal of incorporation into Christ. Jesus through his own baptism identified himself with sinners in order to fulfill all righteousness. Jesus in his own baptism was attested Son by the Father and was anointed with the Holy Spirit to undertake the way of the servant manifested in his sufferings, death, and resurrection. Jesus the risen Lord assured his followers of his continuing presence and power and commissioned them 'Go therefore and make disciples of all nations, baptizing them in the name of the Father and of the Son and of the Holy Spirit, and teaching them to obey everything that I have commanded you. And remember, I am with you always, to the end of the age' (Matt. 28:19).
- W-2.4001 Jesus and the Supper
  - W-2.4001a. Jesus Shared Meals: The Lord's Supper is the sign and seal of eating and drinking in communion with the crucified and risen Lord. During his earthly ministry Jesus shared meals with his

followers as a sign of community and acceptance and as an occasion for his own ministry. He celebrated Israel's feasts of covenant commemoration.

- W-2.4001b. Last Supper: In his last meal before his death Jesus took and shared with his disciples the bread and wine, speaking of them as his body and blood, signs of the new covenant. He commended breaking bread and sharing a cup to remember and proclaim his death.
- W-2.4001c. Resurrection: On the day of his resurrection, the risen Jesus made himself known to his followers in the breaking of bread. He continued to show himself to believers, by blessing and breaking bread, by preparing, serving, and sharing common meals (see also W-1.3033).

4.7. What is the significance (meaning) of each of the sacraments?
  • W-2.3001 Jesus and Baptism: Baptism is the sign and seal of incorporation into Christ.
  • W-2.3002 Dying and Rising in Baptism: In baptism, we participate in Jesus' death and resurrection. In baptism, we die to what separates us from God and are raised to newness of life in Christ. Baptism points us back to the grace of God expressed in Jesus Christ, who died for us and who was raised for us. Baptism points us forward to that same Christ who will fulfill God's purpose in God's promised future.
  • W-2.4001a. The Lord's Supper is the sign and seal of eating and drinking in communion with the crucified and risen Lord.
  • W-2.4004 Remembering: At the Lord's Table, the Church is
    - a. renewed and empowered by the memory of Christ's life, death, resurrection, and promise to return;
    - b. sustained by Christ's pledge of undying love and continuing presence with God's people;
    - c. sealed in God's covenant of grace through partaking of Christ's self-offering.
  • In remembering, believers receive and trust the love of Christ present to them and to the world; they manifest the reality of the covenant of grace in reconciling and being reconciled; and they proclaim the power of Christ's reign for the renewal of the world in justice and in peace.
  • W-2.4006 Communion of the Faithful: Each time they gather at the Table, believing communities
    - a. are united with the Church in every place, and the whole Church is present;
    - b. join with all the faithful in heaven and on earth in offering thanksgiving to the triune God;
    - c. renew the vows taken at baptism;
    - commit themselves afresh to love and serve God, one another, and their neighbors in the world.

4.8. What are some of the ways our worship service integrates Scripture, proclamation, prayer, and praise?
- This question was intended to focus on the order of Service at a particular church. Encourage leaders-elect to try and integrate their understanding of worship by describing how these elements fit together in their particular (Sanctuary or Celebrate) order of worship.

5. Knowledge of Discipline

5.1. What is the purpose of church discipline?
- D-1.0101 Church Discipline: Church discipline is the church's exercise of authority given by Christ, both in the direction of guidance, control, and nurture of its members and in the direction of constructive criticism of offenders. Thus, the purpose of discipline is **to honor God** by making clear the significance of membership in the body of Christ; **to preserve the purity of the church** by nourishing the individual within the life of the believing community; **to correct or restrain wrongdoing** in order to bring members to repentance and restoration; **to restore the unity of the church** by removing the causes of discord and division; and **to secure the just, speedy, and economical determination of proceedings**. In all respects, members are to be accorded procedural safeguards and due process, and it is the intention of these rules so to provide.

5.2. What are the two types of judicial cases?
- D-2.0201 Remedial or Disciplinary: Judicial process consists of two types of cases: remedial and disciplinary.
  - D-2.0202 Remedial: A remedial case is one in which an irregularity (an erroneous decision) or a delinquency (an omission or failure to act) of a lower council, the General Assembly Mission Council, or an entity of the General Assembly may be corrected by a higher council.
  - D-2.0203 Disciplinary: A disciplinary case is one in which a church member or officer may be censured for an offense.

5.3. What is the difference between a dissent and a protest?
- G-3.0105 Dissent: A dissent is a declaration expressing disagreement with a decision of a council. It shall be made at the particular session during which the decision is made. The names of members dissenting shall be recorded.
- G-9.0304 Protest: A protest is a written declaration, supported by reasons, alleging that a decision of a council is or contains an irregularity or a delinquency. Written notice of the protest shall be given at the particular session of the council during which it arose and shall be filed with the clerk before adjournment. If the protest is expressed in

decorous and respectful language, it shall be entered in the minutes of the meeting, and may be accompanied by an answer prepared by the council. No further action is required.

6. Knowledge of This Congregation

NOTE: The answers to these questions are not in the assigned readings. Leaders-elect are instructed to research them on their own.

6.1. When was this church founded? How old is it now?
6.2. How many pastors have served this congregation?
6.3. How many ruling elders and deacons (and trustees) do we have?
6.4. Who is the current clerk of session?
6.5. Who is the current moderator/chair of the Board of Deacons?
6.6. [If your church has trustees] Who is the current chair/moderator of the Trustees?
6.7. What are the major committees (councils, ministries, workgroups, etc.) of the session?
6.8. What are the major committees (councils, ministries, workgroups, etc.) of the Board of Deacons?
6.9. Does this church have a mission statement? If so, what is it?

Constitutional Questions to Officers (W-4.0404)

NOTE: See question 1.5 above. The minister shall ask those preparing to be ordained or installed to stand before the congregation and to answer the following questions:

W-4.0404a. Do you trust in Jesus Christ your Savior, acknowledge him Lord of all and Head of the Church, and through him believe in one God, Father, Son, and Holy Spirit?

W-4.0404b. Do you accept the Scriptures of the Old and New Testaments to be, by the Holy Spirit, the unique and authoritative witness to Jesus Christ in the Church universal, and God's Word to you?

W-4.0404c. Do you sincerely receive and adopt the essential tenets of the Reformed faith as expressed in the confessions of our church as authentic and reliable expositions of what Scripture leads us to believe and do, and will you be instructed and led by those confessions as you lead the people of God?

W-4.0404d.   Will you fulfill your office in obedience to Jesus Christ, under the authority of Scripture, and be continually guided by our confessions?

W-4.0404e.   Will you be governed by our church's polity, and will you abide by its discipline? Will you be a friend among your colleagues in ministry, working with them, subject to the ordering of God's Word and Spirit?

W-4.0404f.   Will you in your own life seek to follow the Lord Jesus Christ, love your neighbors, and work for the reconciliation of the world?

W-4.0404g.   Do you promise to further the peace, unity, and purity of the church?

W-4.0404h.   Will you seek to serve the people with energy, intelligence, imagination, and love?

W-4.0404i (1)   (For ruling elder) Will you be a faithful elder, watching over the people, providing for their worship, nurture, and service? Will you share in government and discipline, serving in councils of the church, and in your ministry will you try to show the love and justice of Jesus Christ?

W-4.0404i (2)   (For deacon) Will you be a faithful deacon, teaching charity, urging concern, and directing the people's help to the friendless and those in need? In your ministry will you try to show the love and justice of Jesus Christ?

Appendix 4

Leader Call Sample Letters

Ruling Elder Call Letter

Dear _____:

Thank you for considering the call to become a **Ruling Elder** at (name of church). As you know, the Nominating Committee has prayerfully considered all persons recommended by members of the congregation. We believe you possess those qualities of discipleship necessary for service as a **Ruling Elder** and that God may be calling you to serve in the **Ruling Elder Class of (Year)**.

The Church's Call

The *Book of Order* of the Presbyterian Church (U.S.A.) describes the ministry of ruling elders in this way:

> As there were in Old Testament times elders for the government of the people, so the New Testament church provided persons with particular gifts to share in discernment of God's Spirit and governance of God's people. Accordingly, congregations should elect persons of wisdom and maturity of faith, having demonstrated skills in leadership and being compassionate in spirit. Ruling elders are so named not because they "lord it over" the congregation (Matt. 20:25) but because they are chosen by the congregation to discern and measure its fidelity to the Word of God and to strengthen and nurture its faith and life. Ruling elders, together with teaching elders, exercise leadership, government, spiritual discernment, and discipline and have responsibilities for the life of a congregation as well as the whole church, including ecumenical relationships.

You may also find it helpful to reflect on Peter's words to elders in Asia Minor in 1 Peter 5:1–4:

> Now an elder myself and a witness of the sufferings of Christ, as well as one who shares in the glory to be revealed, I exhort the elders among you to tend the flock of God that is in yoru charge, exercising the oversight, not under compulsion but willingly, as God would have you do it—not for sordid gain but eagerly. Do not lord it over those in your charge, but be examples to the flock. And when the chief shepherd appears, you will win the crown of glory that never fades away.

Ruling Elder Class of (Year)

(Current Date)

[Page Two]

The Congregation's Call

Accepting the call to service as a Ruling Elder at (church name) includes your commitment to:

- Attend an orientation meeting at the church for newly elected leaders.
    - (date, time).
- Attend all education sessions prior to ordination/installation.
    - Four, three-hour-fifteen-minute sessions (February–April 2015).
    - Three to four hours of homework to prepare for each session.
- Attend all session meetings or request an excused absence.
- Faithfully serve on the Council and/or team to which you are assigned, likely serving in a leadership role (as a chair) for one or more years. Assignments are made by the Assignments Committee based on current needs for the church's ministry.
- Continue to deepen your personal discipleship by regular worship attendance and participation in the mission and ministries of the church.
- Support the church's mission through a pledge of financial support and a commitment to some form of personal ministry.
- Serve Communion in worship on a rotational basis, serving as a lead elder for a Communion team during your second and third years of office.
- Attend presbytery meetings as a commissioner from our session (ordinarily on Tuesdays or Saturdays; typically expected to attend one or two times during each year of the three-year term).
- Answer affirmatively the ordination/installation questions required by our Presbyterian Church (U.S.A.) Constitution.

Preparing for Your Call

Once elected by the congregation, you will become actively involved in a comprehensive program of leader training (see above). This program will include four spiritual formation sessions along with programs on the theology, polity, and "nuts and bolts" of your service in ordained ministry. These programs will be presented by our clergy staff and administered by the Leader Development Team. At the end of your training, you will be examined by the session and then ordained (if not previously ordained) and installed at a Sunday worship service. After this installation service, your term will begin on June 1. Attached is a timetable for these activities.

Ruling Elder Class of (Year)

(Current Date)

[Page Three]

Summary

It is true that accepting a call to God's service is a serious commitment. But it is also a remarkable privilege and opportunity to learn and to deepen your faith and to be blessed in countless ways through leading the people of this congregation in discerning God's will for (church name)'s present and future. You will join men and women who for two thousand years have been called to special duties as the agents of Christ in the church and the world. We are convinced that you will bring your gifts and your dedication, wisdom, faith, and love to the tasks ahead. We are equally convinced that the Holy Spirit will be faithful to you and will equip you for those tasks. Please accept our gratitude for your prayerful consideration of this nomination.

Nominating Committee

(list members)

Attachments

- Important Dates and Responsibilities for New Leaders
- Session and Deacon Ministry Overview
- Ordination/Installation Questions from the *Book of Order*

Accepting the Call

I accept this call to service as a nominee for role of Ruling Elder at _____ Presbyterian Church. I have read this letter and the attachments and have given this commitment prayerful consideration.

Date: _____   _____
(your signature)

Printed Name: _____

(If you accept the call, please date and sign the acceptance. Then please return the signed complete copy of this letter to the Nominating Committee member making the call. Please keep a complete copy for your reference.)

Deacon Call Letter

Dear _____:

Thank you for considering the call to become a **Deacon** at (name of church). As you know, the Nominating Committee has prayerfully considered all persons recommended by members of the congregation. We believe you possess those qualities of discipleship necessary for service as a **Deacon** and that God may be calling you to serve in the Class of (Year).

The Church's Call

The *Book of Order* of the Presbyterian Church (U.S.A.) states some of the duties of Deacons in this way:

> The ministry of deacon as set forth in Scripture is one of compassion, witness, and service, sharing in the redeeming love of Jesus Christ for the poor, the hungry, the sick, the lost, the friendless, the oppressed, those burdened by unjust policies or structures, or anyone in distress. Persons of spiritual character, honest repute, exemplary lives, brotherly and sisterly love, sincere compassion, and sound judgment should be chosen for this ministry.

You may also find it helpful to reflect on Acts 6:1–7 about the first deacons in the Church. The office was instituted out of the need of the local congregation. Many people were being baptized, and the apostles could not keep up with the pastoral care challenges of a growing congregation. Some of the widows in the church were being overlooked in the daily food distribution. In order to continue to build community and not compromise the preaching of the good news, seven people with gifts of compassion, care, and administration were selected to organize the care of the congregation. These first deacons set a pattern for service and ministry to those in need that the church continues to follow.

Deacon Class of (___)

(Current Date)

[Page Two]

The Congregation's Call

Accepting the call to service as a Deacon at (name of church) includes your commitment to:

- Attend all education sessions prior to ordination/installation.
  - Four, three-hour-fifteen-minute sessions (February–April 2015).
  - Three to four hours of homework to prepare for each session.
- Attend all Board of Deacons meetings or request an excused absence.
- Faithfully serve on the committee to which you are appointed.
- Support the Church's mission through a pledge of financial support and a commitment to personal ministry through Every Member Has a Ministry.

Preparing for Your Call

Once elected by the congregation, you will become actively involved in a comprehensive program of leader training. This program will include a series of spiritual formation sessions along with programs on the theology, polity, and "nuts and bolts" of your service as a leader. These programs will be presented by our clergy staff and administered by the Leader Development Team. At the end of your training, you will be examined by the session and then ordained (if not previously ordained) and installed at a Sunday worship service. After this installation service your term will begin. Attached is a timetable for these activities.

Summary

It is true that accepting a call to God's service is a serious commitment. But it is also a remarkable privilege and opportunity to learn and to deepen your faith and to be blessed in countless ways through caring for the people of this congregation. You will join men and women who for two thousand years have been called to special duties as the agents of Christ in the church and the world. We are convinced that you will bring your gifts and your dedication, wisdom, faith, and love to the tasks ahead. We are equally convinced that the Holy Spirit will be faithful to you and will equip you for those tasks. Please accept our gratitude for your prayerful consideration of this nomination.

Deacon Class of (___)

(Current Date)

[Page Three]

Nominating Committee

(list names)

Attachments:

- Important Dates and Responsibilities for New Leaders
- Session and Deacon Ministry Overview
- Ordination/Installation Questions from the *Book of Order*

Accepting the Call

I accept this call to service as a nominee for role of Deacon at
_____ Presbyterian Church. I have read this letter and the
attachments and have given this commitment prayerful consideration.

Date: _____   _____

(your signature)

Printed Name: _____

(If you accept the call, please date and sign the acceptance. Then please return
the signed complete copy of this letter to the Nominating Committee member
making the call. Please keep a complete copy for your reference.)

Appendix 5

Nominating Committee Policies

Manual of Procedure for Nominating and Electing Leaders of (Church Name)

(Church Location)

Revised (date)
Reviewed (date)
Revised (date)

I. Preamble

This revised manual recommended by the Session as of (date) and adopted at a congregational meeting on (date) sets forth the procedure to be followed in the orderly selection of qualified Ruling Elders and Deacons.

II. Leaders, Terms, and Vacancies

1. The Session shall consist of three classes of Ruling Elders. The Nominating Committee shall recommend the total number of Ruling Elders to be determined by the congregation at a congregational meeting.
2. The Board of Deacons shall consist of three classes of Deacons. The Nominating Committee shall recommend the total number of Deacons to be determined by the congregation at a congregational meeting.
3. The customary term of office for Ruling Elder and Deacon shall be three (3) years and, if applicable, for Youth Representatives, one (1) year.
4. The term will typically begin on June 1st of the year elected and ordained and will end on May 31st of the last year of the elected term.

5. A leader may be elected to a subsequent term, but no leader shall serve for consecutive terms, either full or partial, aggregating more than six years. A leader having served six consecutive years shall be ineligible for election for a period of one year.

6. Vacancies in either the Session or Board of Deacons shall be filled at the request of the Clerk of the Session or the Moderator of the Board of Deacons respectively. When possible, vacancies for partial terms will be filled as part of the normal annual nominating process. The congregation shall elect the replacement as soon as possible following a request from the Clerk of Session or the Moderator of the Board of Deacons.

III. Nominating Committee

A Nominating Committee for the nomination of leaders, consisting of active members of the church, shall include both men and women and shall fairly reflect the diversity of the congregation.

1. Members shall be elected annually by the congregation at the annual meeting, customarily to be called for the last Sunday in January.

2. Members customarily shall be elected for a term of one year beginning upon election and shall be eligible to serve three consecutive terms. Continuity in the work of the committee is important. A Pastor will serve as an ex-officio member.

3. The nine members of the Nominating Committee shall consist of:

   a. Session—2 members;

   b. Board of Deacons—2 members;

   c. Congregation—5 members.

4. The members shall be nominated as follows:

   a. Two members from the Session shall be nominated by the Assignments Team as Chair and Vice-Chair of the Nominating Committee.

   b. Two members from the Board of Deacons shall be nominated by the Assignments Team.

   c. Five (5) nominees shall be nominated by the Assignments Team from the Congregation at large, none of whom will be serving as church leaders or employees of the church during their tenure on the Nominating Committee. Nominations may be made from the floor by any active member present. Persons nominated must have given their consent and agreed to serve if elected. From those nominated, the five candidates with the highest number of votes will be elected

5. A vacancy occurring in the Nominating Committee shall be promptly filled by the Assignments Team and shall be confirmed by the Session.

IV. Selection of Nominees

1. The Nominating Committee will prepare and distribute forms to solicit names of potential nominees for Ruling Elder or Deacon from the congregation.
2. Suggestions will be submitted to the Nominating Committee on or before the date set by the Nominating Committee as the deadline for that year.
3. The Nominating Committee shall nominate the number of nominees required to fill the Class of Ruling Elders to be elected and the number of nominees required to fill the Class of Deacons to be elected.
4. Nominees shall not be employees of the Church and shall be involved responsibly in the ministry of the Church as outlined in the Book of Order.

V. Election

1. A congregational meeting shall customarily be called for the 4th Sunday in January and for two succeeding Sundays, if needed, for run-off balloting. The purpose of this meeting is to receive nominations from the committee and from the floor and to elect Ruling Elders and Deacons.
2. Customarily, the Nominating Committee shall present their slate of nominees with pictures and data to the congregation prior to the congregational meeting.
3. After the Nominating Committee presents their slate of leaders for Ruling Elders and Deacons, additional nominations from any active member present can be made from the floor with consent of the nominee who must be able and willing to meet requirements and expectations for ordered ministry.
4. If there are no additional nominations from the congregation, the proposed slate, as presented by the Nominating Committee, will be elected by voice vote.
5. If there are additional nominations from the floor, those names will be written in on spaces provided on the ballot.
6. If there are additional nominations from the floor, the congregation will vote for Ruling Elders and Deacons as presented. A majority of all the voters present and voting shall be required to elect. There will be a run-off balloting on succeeding Sundays, if needed.

VI. Amendments

Amendments to the Manual of Procedure for Nominating and Electing Leaders must be recommended by the Nominating Committee, approved by the Session, and adopted by the congregation at a congregational meeting.

Appendix 6

Opening Worship for Workshops and Seasonal Orders of Worship

Opening Worship for Workshop 1

CALL TO WORSHIP

Leader: The Lord be with you.

People: And also with you.

PRAYER OF CONFESSION

Leader: We bring to God our fears and concerns

All: (individual readings offered in random order)

Note: Participants are asked to write out their fears and concerns in taking office prior to the first session.

ASSURANCE OF PARDON

Leader: In the name of Christ, we are forgiven.

People: Thanks be to God! Amen.

SCRIPTURE: Exodus 3:1–2, 9–15; 4:1–5, 10–17

Moses was keeping the flock of his father-in-law Jethro, the priest of Midian; he led his flock beyond the wilderness, and came to Horeb, the mountain of God. ²There the angel of the LORD appeared to him in a flame of fire out of a bush; he looked, and the bush was blazing, yet it was not consumed. . . .

⁹The cry of the Israelites has now come to me; I have also seen how the Egyptians oppress them. ¹⁰So come, I will send you to Pharaoh to bring my people, the Israelites, out of Egypt." ¹¹But Moses said to God, "Who am I that I should go to Pharaoh, and bring the Israelites out of Egypt?" ¹²He said, "I will be with you; and this shall be the sign for you that it is I who sent you: when you have brought the people out of Egypt, you shall worship God on this mountain."

¹³But Moses said to God, "If I come to the Israelites and say to them, 'The God of your ancestors has sent me to you,' and they ask me, 'What is his name?' what shall I say to them?" ¹⁴God said to Moses, "I AM WHO I AM." He said further, "Thus you shall say to the Israelites, 'I AM has sent me to you.'" ¹⁵God also said to Moses, "Thus you shall say to the Israelites, 'The LORD, the God of your ancestors, the God of Abraham, the God of Isaac, and the God of Jacob, has sent me to you':

This is my name forever,

and this my title for all generations. . . .

4 Then Moses answered, "But suppose they do not believe me or listen to me, but say, 'The LORD did not appear to you.'" ²The LORD said to him, "What is that in your hand?" He said, "A staff." ³And he said, "Throw it on the ground." So he threw the staff on the ground, and it became a snake; and Moses drew back from it. ⁴Then the LORD said to Moses, "Reach out your hand, and seize it by the tail"—so he reached out his hand and grasped it, and it became a staff in his hand—⁵"so that they may believe that the LORD, the God of their ancestors, the God of Abraham, the God of Isaac, and the God of Jacob, has appeared to you." . . .

¹⁰But Moses said to the LORD, "O my Lord, I have never been eloquent, neither in the past nor even now that you have spoken to your servant; but I am slow of speech and slow of tongue." ¹¹Then the LORD said to him, "Who gives speech to mortals? Who makes them mute or deaf, seeing or blind? Is it not I, the LORD? ¹²Now go, and I will be with your mouth and teach you what you are to speak." ¹³But he said, "O my Lord, please send someone else." ¹⁴Then the anger of the LORD was kindled against Moses and he said, "What of your brother Aaron the Levite? I know that he can speak fluently; even now he is coming out to meet you, and when he sees you his heart will be glad. ¹⁵You shall speak to him and put the words in his mouth; and I will be with your mouth and with his mouth, and will teach you what you shall do. ¹⁶He indeed shall speak for you to the people; he shall serve as a mouth for you, and you shall serve as God for him. ¹⁷Take in your hand this staff, with which you shall perform the signs."

REFLECTIONS

BIDDING PRAYERS

Response: Lord, hear our prayer.

COMMUNION

THE PEACE

Opening Worship for Workshop 2

CALL TO WORSHIP

> Leader: The Lord be with you.
>
> **People: And also with you.**

PRAYER OF CONFESSION

> Leader: Lord, I have sinned against you,
> ... in thought *(silence)*,
> ... in word *(silence)*,
> ... in deed *(silence)*.
>
> **All: Hear my prayer and forgive my sin. Renew within me a right spirit, O God. Through Christ we pray. Amen.**

ASSURANCE OF PARDON

> Leader: In the name of Christ, we are forgiven.
>
> **People: Thanks be to God! Amen.**

SCRIPTURE: Numbers 11:10–17

[10]Moses heard the people weeping throughout their families, all at the entrances of their tents. Then the LORD became very angry, and Moses was displeased. [11]So Moses said to the LORD, "Why have you treated your servant so badly? Why have I not found favor in your sight, that you lay the burden of all this people on me? [12]Did I conceive all this people? Did I give birth to them, that you should say to me, 'Carry them in your bosom, as a nurse carries a sucking child to the land that you promised on oath to their ancestors'? [13]Where am I to get meat to give all this people? For they come weeping to me and say, 'Give us meat to eat!' [14]I am not able to carry all this people alone, for they are too heavy for me. [15]If this is the way you are going to treat me, put me to death at once—if I have found favor in your sight—and do not let me see my misery."

[16]So the LORD said to Moses, "Gather for me seventy of the elders of Israel, whom you know to be the elders of the people and officers over them; bring them to the tent of meeting, and have them take their place there with you. [17]I will come down and talk with you there; and I will take some of the spirit that is on you and put it on them; and they shall bear

the burden of the people along with you so that you will not bear it all by yourself.

REFLECTIONS

BIDDING PRAYERS

Response: Lord, hear our prayer.

COMMUNION

THE PEACE

Opening Worship for Workshop 3

CALL TO WORSHIP

> Leader: The Lord be with you.
>
> **People: And also with you.**

HYMN: "Let Us Break Bread Together" [513 (PH) / 525 (GTG)]

PRAYER OF CONFESSION

> Leader: God has chosen you to be a leader in the Church.
>
> **Elders: Ruling elders are "persons of wisdom and maturity of faith, having demonstrated skills in leadership and being compassionate in spirit" (G-2.0301).**
>
> **Deacons: Deacons should be "persons of spiritual character, honest repute, exemplary lives, brotherly and sisterly love, sincere compassion, and sound judgment" (G-2.0201).**
>
> Leader: Where is your weakness in being this person? In silence, confess your sin to God and ask God to strengthen you for service. *(Silence.)*

ASSURANCE OF PARDON

> Leader: Have you not known? Have you not heard? The Lord is the everlasting God, the Creator of the ends of the earth. He does not faint or grow weary; his understanding is unsearchable. He gives power to the faint and strengthens the powerless (see Isa. 40:28–29).
>
> **People: In the name of Jesus Christ our sins are forgiven!**
>
> **All: Thanks be to God! Amen.**

SCRIPTURE: Mark 6:30–44

> Narrator: The apostles gathered around Jesus, and told him all that they had done and taught. He said to them,
>
> Jesus: Come away to a deserted place all by yourselves and rest a while.

Narrator: For many were coming and going, and they had no leisure even to eat. And they went away in the boat to a deserted place by themselves. Now many saw them going and recognized them, and they hurried there on foot from all the towns and arrived ahead of them. As he went ashore, he saw a great crowd; and he had compassion for them, because they were like sheep without a shepherd; and he began to teach them many things. When it grew late, his disciples came to him and said,

Disciples: This is a deserted place, and the hour is now very late; send them away so that they may go into the surrounding country and villages and buy something for themselves to eat.

Narrator: But he answered them,

Jesus: You give them something to eat.

Narrator: They said to him,

Disciples: Are we to go and buy two hundred denarii worth of bread, and give it to them to eat?

Narrator: And he said to them,

Jesus: How many loaves have you? Go and see.

Narrator: When they had found out, they said,

Disciples: Five, and two fish.

Narrator: Then he ordered them to get all the people to sit down in groups on the green grass. So they sat down in groups of hundreds and of fifties. Taking the five loaves and the two fish, he looked up to heaven, and blessed and broke the loaves, and gave them to his disciples to set before the people; and he divided the two fish among them all. And all ate and were filled; and they took up twelve baskets full of broken pieces and of the fish. Those who had eaten the loaves numbered five thousand men.

REFLECTIONS

BIDDING PRAYERS

Response: Lord, hear our prayer.

COMMUNION

THE PEACE

Opening Worship for Workshop 4

CALL TO WORSHIP

> Leader: The Lord be with you.
>
> **People: And also with you.**

HYMN *(SEATED)*: "Come, Holy Spirit, Heavenly Dove"
[126 (PH) / 279 (GTG)]

SILENT CONFESSION

ASSURANCE OF PARDON

> Leader: Hear the Good News!
>
> **People: In Jesus Christ our sins are forgiven!**

SCRIPTURE *(UNISON)*: Ephesians 4:11–16

[11]The gifts he gave were that some would be apostles, some prophets, some evangelists, some pastors and teachers, [12]to equip the saints for the work of ministry, for building up the body of Christ, [13]until all of us come to the unity of the faith and of the knowledge of the Son of God, to maturity, to the measure of the full stature of Christ. [14]We must no longer be children, tossed to and fro and blown about by every wind of doctrine, by people's trickery, by their craftiness in deceitful scheming. [15]But speaking the truth in love, we must grow up in every way into him who is the head, into Christ, [16]from whom the whole body, joined and knit together by every ligament with which it is equipped, as each part is working properly, promotes the body's growth in building itself up in love.

REFLECTIONS

BIDDING PRAYERS

> **Response: Lord, hear our prayer.**

COMMUNION

THE PEACE

Seasonal Orders of Worship

Advent

CALL TO WORSHIP

HYMN: "O Come, O Come, Emmanuel" [9 (PH) / 88 (GTG)]

PRAYER OF CONFESSION *(UNISON)*

Lord, we long for the wrong things. We toil and labor but often in the wrong kingdom. We place our hope in lesser gods, and we live without expectation of your coming.

In your mercy, forgive us. Grant us a vision of the truth. Inspire us to love and serve you with all of our heart, mind, and strength. Through Christ we pray. Amen.

DECLARATION OF PARDON

SCRIPTURE: Luke 3:1–6

In the fifteenth year of the reign of Emperor Tiberius, when Pontius Pilate was governor of Judea, and Herod was ruler of Galilee, and his brother Philip ruler of the region of Ituraea and Trachonitis, and Lysanias ruler of Abilene, [2]during the high priesthood of Annas and Caiaphas, the word of God came to John son of Zechariah in the wilderness. [3]He went into all the region around the Jordan, proclaiming a baptism of repentance for the forgiveness of sins, [4]as it is written in the book of the words of the prophet Isaiah,
    "The voice of one crying out in the wilderness:
    'Prepare the way of the Lord,
        make his paths straight.
    [5]Every valley shall be filled,
        and every mountain and hill shall be made low,
    and the crooked shall be made straight,
        and the rough ways made smooth;
    [6]and all flesh shall see the salvation of God.'"

REFLECTIONS

BIDDING PRAYERS

Response: Lord, hear our prayer.

COMMUNION *(INTINCTION)*

THE PEACE

Beginning of the New Year

CALL TO WORSHIP

HYMN: "Guide Me, O Thou Great Jehovah" [281 (PH) / 65 (GTG)]

PRAYER OF CONFESSION (*UNISON*)

God of grace, we are weak, but you are strong. We are prone to sin, but you are holy. We are limited in our vision, but you see and know all things. Forgive us for the many ways we offend you. Heal our hearts and minds and guide us as we lead your people. Through Christ we pray. Amen.

ASSURANCE OF PARDON

SCRIPTURE: Luke 10:25–37

[25]Just then a lawyer stood up to test Jesus. "Teacher," he said, "what must I do to inherit eternal life?" [26]He said to him, "What is written in the law? What do you read there?" [27]He answered, "You shall love the Lord your God with all your heart, and with all your soul, and with all your strength, and with all your mind; and your neighbor as yourself." [28]And he said to him, "You have given the right answer; do this, and you will live."

[29]But wanting to justify himself, he asked Jesus, "And who is my neighbor?" [30]Jesus replied, "A man was going down from Jerusalem to Jericho, and fell into the hands of robbers, who stripped him, beat him, and went away, leaving him half dead. [31]Now by chance a priest was going down that road; and when he saw him, he passed by on the other side. [32]So likewise a Levite, when he came to the place and saw him, passed by on the other side. [33]But a Samaritan while traveling came near him; and when he saw him, he was moved with pity. [34]He went to him and bandaged his wounds, having poured oil and wine on them. Then he put him on his own animal, brought him to an inn, and took care of him. [35]The next day he took out two denarii, gave them to the innkeeper, and said, 'Take care of him; and when I come back, I will repay you whatever more you spend.' [36]Which of these three, do you think, was a neighbor to the man who fell into the hands of the robbers?" [37]He said, "The one who showed him mercy." Jesus said to him, "Go and do likewise."

REFLECTIONS

BIDDING PRAYERS

Response: Lord, hear our prayer.

COMMUNION *(INTINCTION)*

THE PEACE

Lent

CALL TO WORSHIP

> Leader: The Lord be with you.
>
> **People: And also with you.**

HYMN *(SEATED)*: "Come, Holy Spirit, Heavenly Dove" [126 (PH) / 279 (GTG)]

LITANY OF PENITENCE*

> Leader: Let us pray.
>
> **All: Holy and merciful God,**
> **we confess to you and to one another,**
> **and to the whole communion of saints in heaven and on earth,**
> **that we have sinned by our own fault**
> **in thought, word, and deed,**
> **by what we have done,**
> **and by what we have left undone.**
>
> Leader: We have not loved you with our whole heart, and mind, and strength.
> We have not loved our neighbors as ourselves.
> We have not forgiven others as we have been forgiven.
>
> **People: Have mercy on us, O God.**
>
> Leader: We have not listened to your call to serve as Christ served us.
> We have not been true to the mind of Christ.
> We have grieved your Holy Spirit.
>
> **People: Have mercy on us, O God.**
>
> Leader: We confess to you, O God, all our past unfaithfulness:
> the pride, hypocrisy, and impatience in our lives,
>
> **People: we confess to you, O God.**
>
> Leader: Our self-indulgent appetites and ways
> and our exploitation of other people,
>
> **People: we confess to you, O God.**

*The Litany of Penitence is from *Book of Common Worship* (Louisville, KY: Westminster/ John Knox Press, 1993), 225–26.

Leader: Our anger at our own frustration
and our envy of those more fortunate than ourselves,

People: we confess to you, O God.

Leader: Our intemperate love of worldly goods and comforts,
and our dishonesty in daily life and work,

People: we confess to you, O God.

Leader: Our negligence in prayer and worship,
and our failure to commend the faith that is in us,

People: we confess to you, O God.

Leader: Accept our repentance, O God,
for the wrongs we have done.
for our neglect of human need and suffering
and our indifference to injustice and cruelty,

People: accept our repentance, O God.

Leader: For all false judgments,
for uncharitable thoughts toward our neighbors,
and for our prejudice and contempt
toward those who differ from us,

People: accept our repentance, O God.

Leader: For our waste and pollution of your creation
and our lack of concern for those who come after us,

People: accept our repentance, O God.

Leader: Restore us, O God,
and let your anger depart from us.

**All: Favorably hear us, O God,
for your mercy is great. Amen.**

ASSURANCE OF PARDON

Leader: Hear the Good News!

People: In Jesus Christ our sins are forgiven!

SCRIPTURE *(UNISON)*: Ephesians 4:11–16

[11]The gifts he gave were that some would be apostles, some prophets, some evangelists, some pastors and teachers, [12]to equip the saints for the work of ministry, for building up the body of Christ, [13]until all of us come to the unity of the faith and of the knowledge of the Son of God, to maturity, to the measure of the full stature of Christ. [14]We must no longer be children, tossed to and fro and blown about by every wind of doctrine, by people's trickery, by their craftiness in deceitful scheming. [15]But speaking the truth in love, we must grow up in every way into him who is the head, into Christ, [16]from whom the whole body, joined and knit together by every ligament with which it is equipped, as each part is working properly, promotes the body's growth in building itself up in love.

REFLECTIONS

BIDDING PRAYERS

Response: Lord, hear our prayer.

COMMUNION *(INTINCTION)*

THE PEACE.

Pentecost

CALL TO WORSHIP

>   Leader: The Lord be with you.

>   **People: And also with you.**

HYMN *(SEATED)*: "Breathe on Me, Breath of God"
[316 (PH) / 286 (GTG)]

PRAYER OF CONFESSION

>   Leader: Lord, if I were to be your faithful disciple, what would have to change in my life? *(Silence.)*

ASSURANCE OF PARDON

>   Leader: Hear the Good News!

>   **People: In Jesus Christ our sins are forgiven!**

SCRIPTURE: *(UNISON)* Acts 1:8, 2:1–4, 43–47

[8]"But you will receive power when the Holy Spirit has come upon you; and you will be my witnesses in Jerusalem, in all Judea and Samaria, and to the ends of the earth." . . .

2 When the day of Pentecost had come, they were all together in one place. [2]And suddenly from heaven there came a sound like the rush of a violent wind, and it filled the entire house where they were sitting. [3]Divided tongues, as of fire, appeared among them, and a tongue rested on each of them. [4]All of them were filled with the Holy Spirit and began to speak in other languages, as the Spirit gave them ability. . . .

[43]Awe came upon everyone, because many wonders and signs were being done by the apostles. [44]All who believed were together and had all things in common; [45]they would sell their possessions and goods and distribute the proceeds to all, as any had need.[46]Day by day, as they spent much time together in the temple, they broke bread at home and ate their food with glad and generous hearts, [47]praising God and having the goodwill of all the people. And day by day the Lord added to their number those who were being saved.

REFLECTIONS

BIDDING PRAYERS

Response: Lord, hear our prayer.

COMMUNION *(INTINCTION)*

THE PEACE

Independence Day

CALL TO WORSHIP

HYMN: "My Country, 'Tis of Thee" [561 (PH) / 337 (GTG)]

PRAYER OF CONFESSION *(UNISON)*

God of all creation, forgive, we pray, the sins of our nation: our racism, discrimination, prejudice, and pride. Forgive our neglect of the poor and worship of the rich. Forgive our abuse of the environment and the gifts of your creation.

Purify our hearts; grant us wisdom and restore us to the joy of your salvation. Through Christ, the risen Lord, we pray. Amen.

ASSURANCE OF PARDON

SCRIPTURE *(PRINT COPIES AND INVITE OTHERS TO READ)*

   2 Chronicles 7:11–16
   Psalm 8
   Proverbs 3:5–6
   Isaiah 40:28–31
   Jeremiah 29:11–14

PRAYER

   Leader: Almighty God,
      you have given us this good land as our heritage.

   **People: Make us always remember your generosity
      and constantly do your will.**

   Leader: Bless our land with honest industry,
      sound learning,
      and an honorable way of life.

   **People: Save us from violence, discord, and confusion;
      from pride and arrogance;
      and from every evil way.**

Leader: Make us who come from many nations
with many different languages
a united people.

**People: Defend our liberties and give those whom
we have entrusted with the authority of government
the spirit of wisdom, that there might be justice and
peace in our land.**

Leader: When times are prosperous, let our hearts be thankful;
and, in troubled times, do not let our trust in you fail.

**All: We ask all this through Jesus Christ our Lord, who taught
us to pray:**

**Our Father, who art in heaven, hallowed be thy name.
Thy kingdom come, thy will be done, on earth as it is in
heaven.
Give us this day our daily bread;
and forgive us our debts, as we forgive our debtors;
and lead us not into temptation, but deliver us from evil.
For thine is the kingdom and the power and the glory,
forever. Amen**

REFLECTIONS

COMMUNION *(INTINCTION)*

THE PEACE

Stewardship Season

CALL TO WORSHIP

HYMN *(SEATED)*: "Take My Life" [391 (PH) / 697 (GTG)]

> Verse 1 Take my life, and let it be Consecrated, Lord, to Thee.
> Take my moments and my days; Let them flow in ceaseless praise,
> Let them flow in ceaseless praise.

SILENT CONFESSION AND PARDON

HYMN *(SEATED)*

> Verse 2 Take my hands, and let them move At the impulse of Thy love.
> Take my feet, and let them be Swift and beautiful for Thee,
> Swift and beautiful for Thee.

OT READING: Psalm 116:12–19

> 12What shall I return to the LORD
>   for all his bounty to me?
> 13I will lift up the cup of salvation
>   and call on the name of the LORD,
> 14I will pay my vows to the LORD
>   in the presence of all his people.
> 15Precious in the sight of the LORD
>   is the death of his faithful ones.
> 16O LORD, I am your servant;
>   I am your servant, the child of your serving girl.
>   You have loosed my bonds.
> 17I will offer to you a thanksgiving sacrifice
>   and call on the name of the LORD.
> 18I will pay my vows to the LORD
>   in the presence of all his people,
> 19in the courts of the house of the LORD,
>   in your midst, O Jerusalem.
> Praise the LORD!

HYMN *(SEATED)*

> Verse 3 Take my voice, and let me sing, Always, only, for my King.
> Take my lips, and let them be Filled with messages from Thee,
> Filled with messages from Thee.

NT READING: Matthew 22:15–22

[15]Then the Pharisees went and plotted to entrap him in what he said. [16]So they sent their disciples to him, along with the Herodians, saying, "Teacher, we know that you are sincere, and teach the way of God in accordance with truth, and show deference to no one; for you do not regard people with partiality. [17]Tell us, then, what you think. Is it lawful to pay taxes to the emperor, or not?" [18]But Jesus, aware of their malice, said, "Why are you putting me to the test, you hypocrites? [19]Show me the coin used for the tax." And they brought him a denarius. [20]Then he said to them, "Whose head is this, and whose title?" [21]They answered, "The emperor's." Then he said to them, "Give therefore to the emperor the things that are the emperor's, and to God the things that are God's." [22]When they heard this, they were amazed; and they left him and went away.

HYMN *(SEATED)*

> Verse 4 Take my silver and my gold. Not a mite would I withhold;
> Take my intellect, and use Every power as Thou shalt choose,
> Every power as Thou shalt choose.

PRAYERS

HYMN *(SEATED)*

> Verse 5 Take my will, and make it Thine; It shall be no longer mine.
> Take my heart, it is Thine own; It shall be Thy royal throne,
> It shall be Thy royal throne.

COMMUNION *(INTINCTION)*

HYMN *(SEATED)*

> Verse 6 Take my love; my Lord, I pour At thy feet its treasure store.
> Take myself, and I will be Ever, only, all for Thee,
> Ever, only, all for Thee.

THE PEACE

Thanksgiving

CALL TO WORSHIP

HYMN: "We Gather Together" [559 (PH) / 336 (GTG)]

Verse 1   We gather together to ask the Lord's blessing;
He chastens and hastens His will to make known;
The wicked oppressing now cease from distressing,
Sing praises to His name; He forgets not His own.

SCRIPTURE: Psalm 100

¹Make a joyful noise to the LORD, all the earth.
²Worship the LORD with gladness;
come into his presence with singing.

³Know that the LORD is God.
It is he that made us, and we are his;
we are his people, and the sheep of his pasture.

⁴Enter his gates with thanksgiving,
and his courts with praise.
Give thanks to him, bless his name.

⁵For the LORD is good;
his steadfast love endures forever,
and his faithfulness to all generations.

PRAYERS OF THANKSGIVING—FOR THE NATION (BIDDING PRAYERS)

HYMN

Verse 2   Beside us to guide us, our God with us joining,
Ordaining, maintaining His kingdom divine;
So from the beginning the fight we were winning;
Thou, Lord, wast at our side; All glory be Thine!

SCRIPTURE: Philippians 4:4–9

⁴Rejoice in the Lord always; again I will say, Rejoice. ⁵Let your gentleness be known to everyone. The Lord is near. ⁶Do not worry about anything, but in everything by prayer and supplication with thanksgiving let your

requests be made known to God. [7]And the peace of God, which surpasses all understanding, will guard your hearts and your minds in Christ Jesus.

[8]Finally, beloved, whatever is true, whatever is honorable, whatever is just, whatever is pure, whatever is pleasing, whatever is commendable, if there is any excellence and if there is anything worthy of praise, think about these things. [9]Keep on doing the things that you have learned and received and heard and seen in me, and the God of peace will be with you.

PRAYERS OF THANKSGIVING—FOR FAMILIES

HYMN

> Verse 3   We all do extol Thee, Thou leaders triumphant,
> And pray that Thou still our defender wilt be.
> Let Thy congregation escape tribulation;
> Thy name be ever praised! O Lord, make us free!

SCRIPTURE: John 6:25–35

[25]When they found him on the other side of the sea, they said to him, "Rabbi, when did you come here?" [26]Jesus answered them, "Very truly, I tell you, you are looking for me, not because you saw signs, but because you ate your fill of the loaves. [27]Do not work for the food that perishes, but for the food that endures for eternal life, which the Son of Man will give you. For it is on him that God the Father has set his seal." [28]Then they said to him, "What must we do to perform the works of God?" [29]Jesus answered them, "This is the work of God, that you believe in him whom he has sent." [30]So they said to him, "What sign are you going to give us then, so that we may see it and believe you? What work are you performing? [31]Our ancestors ate the manna in the wilderness; as it is written, 'He gave them bread from heaven to eat.'" [32]Then Jesus said to them, "Very truly, I tell you, it was not Moses who gave you the bread from heaven, but it is my Father who gives you the true bread from heaven. [33]For the bread of God is that which comes down from heaven and gives life to the world." [34]They said to him, "Sir, give us this bread always."

[35]Jesus said to them, "I am the bread of life. Whoever comes to me will never be hungry, and whoever believes in me will never be thirsty.

PRAYERS OF THANKSGIVING—FOR THE CHURCH

COMMUNION (INTINCTION)

THE PEACE

A Service of Wholeness

NOTE: The congregation is invited to join the group for this special service.

CALL TO WORSHIP

HYMN: "Our God, Our Help in Ages Past" [210 (PH) / 687 (GTG)]

PRAYER OF CONFESSION *(UNISON)*

Merciful God,
we confess that we have sinned against you
in thought, word, and deed,
by what we have done,
and by what we have left undone.
We have not loved you
with our whole heart and mind and strength;
we have not loved our neighbors as ourselves.
In your mercy forgive what we have been,
help us amend what we are,
and direct what we shall be,
so that we may delight in your will
and walk in your ways,
to the glory of your holy name.

ASSURANCE OF PARDON

SCRIPTURE: James 5:13–16

[13]Are any among you suffering? They should pray. Are any cheerful? They should sing songs of praise. [14]Are any among you sick? They should call for the elders of the church and have them pray over them, anointing them with oil in the name of the Lord. [15]The prayer of faith will save the sick, and the Lord will raise them up; and anyone who has committed sins will be forgiven. [16]Therefore confess your sins to one another, and pray for one another, so that you may be healed. The prayer of the righteous is powerful and effective.

REFLECTIONS

INTERCESSION FOR HEALING[*]

Leader: God, our creator,
your will for us and for all your people
is health and salvation:

People: have mercy on us.

Leader: Jesus Christ, Son of God,
you came that we might have life
and have it in abundance:

People: have mercy on us.

Leader: Holy Spirit,
dwelling within us,
you make us temples in your presence:

People: have mercy on us.

Leader: To the triune God,
the source of all love and all life,
let us offer our prayers.
For all who are in need of healing,

Silence

Lord, in your mercy,

People: hear our prayer.

Leader: For all who are disabled by injury or illness,

Silence

Lord, in your mercy,

People: hear our prayer.

Leader: For all who are troubled by confusion or pain,

Silence

Lord, in your mercy,

People: hear our prayer.

Leader: For all whose increasing years bring weariness,

Silence

Lord, in your mercy,

People: hear our prayer.

Leader: For all about to undergo surgery,

Silence

Lord, in your mercy,

People: hear our prayer.

Leader: For all who cannot sleep,

Silence

Lord, in your mercy,

People: hear our prayer.

Leader: For all who practice the healing arts,

Silence

Lord, in your mercy,

People: hear our prayer.

Leader: Here petitions for specific needs may be offered by the people.
Into your hands, O God,
we commend all for whom we pray,
trusting in your mercy;
through Jesus Christ our Lord.

All: Amen.

LAYING OF HANDS AND ANOINTING WITH OIL

As persons enter the circle and receive prayer, the leaders anoint them with oil and say, "We anoint you in the name of the Father, the Son, and the Holy Spirit. Amen."

BENEDICTION

BLESSING AND THE PEACE

*The Intercession for Healing litany is from *Book of Common Worship* (Louisville, KY: Westminster/John Knox Press, 1993), 1005–15.

Appendix 7

Leadership Texts for Worship

*T*hese texts speak to leadership.

Text	Theme
Genesis 12:1–9	The call of Abram/Sarai
Genesis 22:1–18	The test of Abraham
Exodus 3:1–14	The call of Moses
Exodus 14:10–31	The Red Sea
Exodus 16	The manna
Exodus 18	Jethro's advice
Exodus 32	The golden calf
Exodus 33:7–23	The tent of meeting
Numbers 11:4–17	The seventy elders
Deuteronomy 8:10–20	Don't forget
Judges 6	Gideon—being reduced
1 Samuel 16	The call of David
2 Chronicles 7:11–16	"If my people…"
Psalm 51	The sins of leadership
Ecclesiastes 3:1–18	Timing
Jeremiah 32:1–15	Jeremiah's field
Micah 6:8	What does the Lord require?
Malachi 3:6–12	The tithe
Matthew 4:1–11	The temptation of Jesus
Matthew 8:18–22	The cost of discipleship

(*continued on the next page*)

Text	Theme
Matthew 10:1–42	Sending the Twelve
Matthew 13:24–30	The Parable of the Weeds
Matthew 19:16–30	The Rich Young Man
Mark 4:1–20	The Parable of the Sower
Mark 6:30–44	Feeding of five thousand
Luke 5:17–26	The healing of a paralytic
Luke 10:38–42	Mary and Martha
Luke 21:1–4	The widow's example
Luke 24:1–12	The resurrection
John 3:1–21	Nicodemus
John 15:1–17	The vine and the branches
Acts 2	Pentecost
Acts 7:54–60	The stoning of Stephen
Acts 9:1–9	Saul's conversion
Ephesians 4:1–16	The offices of leadership
1 Timothy 3:1–13	Qualifications for the offices
James 5:13–16	Prayer

Appendix 8

Using Case Studies

Case studies allow learners to deal with real-life situations while remaining one step removed. It is often much easier to asses and critically reflect on the issues and dynamics of a conflict, problem, or challenge if you are not right in the middle of it. Case study scenarios are used in the standard ordination exams for teaching elders. They also can be helpful resources in your preparation of ruling elders and deacons for service in ordered ministry. There is one case study in Workshop 3.

Each case study consists of some situation taken from life in the church. Most were prompted by actual experiences. Some have been creatively enhanced to make a better teaching activity. The case presents a scenario and asks the leader (usually a ruling elder) to take some action or make some response to the scenario. Leaders are invited to define the problem, reflect on what is at stake in theology and polity, and to research the appropriate guidance in the Constitution. Finally, using all this and their pastoral sensitivities, they are invited to say what they would actually do in response.

Processing the case will give leaders practical experience in applying Presbyterian / Reformed principles to real-life situations. Leaders will learn what difference our polity and theology make in our personal and corporate lives.

General Guidelines for Using Case Studies

Here is a general way to use the case studies (30–45 minutes):

1. Review the case and do your own research on the questions and issues presented.
    a. Prepare any supplemental resources that might be useful (e.g. compilations of constitutional references).

2. Distribute the case study in advance to participants for individual reading and reflection on the questions posed.
3. Use the large group to review the case, that is, go over the situation to clarify any questions.
4. Invite participants to talk through the case and respond to the questions posed in a large group or in smaller groupings.
5. Bring everyone together to share and discuss their responses.

Ways to Use Case Studies in Leader Development

Below are ways to incorporate the case study resources into your leader development program.

As a Replacement for a Workshop Worksheet

After you've had some experience using a worksheet (multiple years of use or you just don't like it for whatever reason), substitute one of the case studies and build the lesson around it. Workshop #3 uses a case study, so you can use that teaching activity as a guide.

As Continuing Education for Church Leaders

Most leader development programs in church end when a ruling elder or deacon is installed to service in ordered ministry. In order to foster growth and development over the three years of a leader's service, consider using the case studies as opportunities for continuing education.

Offer an optional thirty-minute opportunity to process a case right before a session or Board of Deacons meeting. Instead of monthly case studies, spread them out—once a quarter, or a short series in the fall, winter, or spring. If you distribute the cases in advance, and not everyone attends the discussion, be prepared for leaders wanting to know the "answers." Case studies draw people in.

Create Your Own

Writing your own case studies can be an act of creative expression for you as teaching elder. It can also be a way of preparing your leaders for potential issues and challenges not yet a part of their experience.

Pick topics that are not current hot issues. Cases too close to current issues can devolve into advocacy and defensiveness. Use situations from your past experience in the church. Ask your colleagues for suggested topics. Start with an important principle and imagine a scenario that would highlight it.

Case Studies Provided in the *Participant Workbook*

The chart below provides an index of case studies provided in the *Participant Workbook*, along with the topics they address. These may give some suggestions for where a particular case might be useful. You may see other connections.

#	Title	Topics
1	Maintaining the Purity of the Church (located in Workshop 3)	Dilemma of what to do after discovering unethical behavior by a potential church leader nominee.
2	Baptism, Pastoral Sensitivity, and Polity	Private baptism, godparents, baptizing children from another congregation.
3	The Mission Budget	Who votes on the budget? Majority rule.
4	Left Behind in the Rapture	Rapture theology, Presbyterian views on the end times.
5	Member, Member, Who's a Member?	Criteria for membership; purging the rolls, per-capita apportionment.
6	Calvin Presbyterian Church	How to disagree with church actions; when you don't get your way.
7	Predestination	What do Presbyterians believe about predestination?
8	Charlotte, Worship, and the Body of Christ	Caring for the whole church; distractions in worship.
9	Believe It or Not	What do Presbyterians believe about the Bible, its authority, and interpretation?
10	Baptizing Baby Bobby	Pastoral vs. polity: Who can present a child for baptism?
11	Meetings, Committees, and the Presbyterian Way	Getting commissioners to presbytery meetings; responsibilities of ruling elders; inefficiency of committees.
12	Church Membership—Easy or Hard?	Criteria for church membership: Who sets the standards and how?

(*continued on the next page*)

#	Title	Topics
13	What Age Communion?	Should children take Communion? Shouldn't they understand what it means?
14	Christians and Jews	Religious tolerance; Presbyterian stance on evangelizing to Jews; sharing worship space.
15	Pastoral or Polity?	Pastoral care for all members; blessing a homosexual relationship.
16	In the Beginning . . .	Evolution; Presbyterians and public schools. Are the biblical creation stories meant to be take literally?
17	The Will of God	Pastoral care vs. theology: Is everything that happens the will of God?
18	God Shed His Grace on Thee	Flags in the sanctuary; patriotism and Christian worship.
19	A Majority of Dissent	Advocacy in the Presbyterian system: an orderly way to change things.
20	Local Option	Ordination and homosexual nominees.
21	The Presbyterian Way to Worship	Alternate forms of worship: Is there a Presbyterian style of worship?
22	The Essential Tenets	What do Presbyterian leaders have to believe? Is belief in the virgin birth essential?

Appendix 9

Other Resources
for Church Leader Development

Websites

www.openingdoorstodiscipleship.com also odtd.net

Developed by five reformed denominations in North America, *Opening Doors to Discipleship* provides a series of four online courses in the Presbyterian/Reformed tradition to equip teachers and leaders. The four courses are *Teaching Skills, Bible Background, Presbyterian/Reformed Faith,* and *Discipleship.* Each course has twelve sessions. The online learning model works with individuals as self-paced instruction but is better suited for a group of leaders learning together. PC(USA) congregations, once registered, will have free access to all courses. Register your congregation online.

www.pcusa.org

The denomination's website has a rich collection of resources to help inform and educate your leaders. There you will find downloadable copies of the *Book of Order, Book of Confessions,* catechisms, updates on global and national mission, and commentary on the church's actions. In the "Who We Are" section you'll find videos on Presbyterian polity, brief summaries of Presbyterian beliefs and practices, how we are governed, how we are organized, and the history of the PC(USA).

www.pcusastore.com

This comes from the Presbyterian Publishing Corporation—the same folks who provide resources at www.TheThoughtfulChristian.com— developed *by* Presbyterians *for* Presbyterians, to provide the inspiration and the information necessary to cultivate new congregational leaders and support existing ones. Some resources are available free (Presbyterian social witness statements and a series of Leading Voices essays) while others are available for a fee. Note especially the section on Leadership, which has excellent modules for leadership development of persons in ordered ministry.

www.pres-outlook.com

The Presbyterian Outlook is a bi-weekly publication providing "leaders and future leaders a trusted source of accurate reporting, insightful analysis, thought-provoking commentaries and congregational resources" (from the website). Consider providing your leaders with a yearly subscription to the print or electronic version to keep them up to date on the PC(USA)! The free online version has news articles, analysis, and opinion pieces to keep your leaders informed about the larger church. A number of articles in each current are available for free on the website and can be e-mailed as links to your leaders.

www.theocademy.com

Theocademy is a project of the Synod of Mid-America in partnership with other synods, organizations, and seminaries. There are two current video series, one for new members and the other for ruling elders and deacons. This one has great usefulness for leadership development. The videos are free and accessible from the website. You can view the videos from the site and download a study guide for free. You may also purchase a set of DVDs ($10 per four sessions).

General Books / Resources

Constitution

Presbyterian Polity for Church Leaders. Fourth Edition. Joan S. Gray and Joyce C. Tucker. Louisville, KY: Geneva Press, 2012.

This is an in-depth and comprehensive interpretation of the *Book of Order* and the basics of Presbyterian polity following the adoption of the new Form of Government in 2011. The book provides historical background, a summary of content, and contemporary commentary on the Presbyterian way of doing things.

Selected to Serve: A Guide for Church Leaders. Second Edition. Earl S. Johnson Jr. Louisville, KY: Geneva Press, 2012.

This is a great handbook and text for church officer training and is used in our workshop model. Easy to read text with study questions covers the typical issues leaders face and the content required for examination. Chapters provide overviews of governance, worship, discipline, the confessions, ordination vows, ethical and professional standards, and helping your church to grow. Scriptural, constitutional, and general indices make for easy reference.

Leadership

Sailboat Church: Helping Your Church Rethink Its Mission and Practice. Joan S. Gray. Louisville, KY: Westminster John Knox Press, 2014.

The church should be a "sailboat" guided and powered by the Holy Spirit—not a "rowboat" dependent on human effort. Gray provides forty days of sailing prayers, Scripture references, and reflection questions designed to help leaders reframe their church's mission and practice.

Spiritual Leadership for Church Officers: A Handbook. Joan S. Gray. Louisville, KY: Geneva Press, 2009.

(From publisher's description:) This leadership guide is written for church leaders who are looking for a deepened relationship with God as they serve the church. Ruling elders and deacons are challenged to see themselves as spiritual leaders serving alongside their pastors. The author lays out a variety of leadership styles and helps leaders understand when each might be appropriate. The book provides resources for dealing with interpersonal relationships in the church and identifies ways churches can create an atmosphere that is supportive of the spiritual leadership of ruling elders and deacons.

The Presbyterian Ruling Elder: An Essential Guide. Paul S. Wright, revised by Stephen G. Lynch. Louisville, KY: Westminster John Knox Press, 2014.

This revision updates the classic booklet, providing a simple, brief overview of the role and responsibilities of ruling elders.

The Presbyterian Deacon: an Essential Guide. Earl S. Johnson Jr. Louisville, KY: Westminster John Knox Press, 2014.

This revised booklet provides a brief overview of the role and responsibilities of deacons in their varied ministries in congregations.

Presbyterian Beliefs

Being Presbyterian in the Bible Belt: A Theological Survival Guide for Youth, Parents, and Other Confused Presbyterians. Ted V. Foote Jr. and P. Alex Thornburg. Louisville, KY: Westminster John Knox Press, 2000.

This simple and slightly irreverent (humorous) book tackles questions from popular culture (e.g., Are you saved or are you a Presbyterian?) and answers them from a thoroughly Reformed/Presbyterian perspective. Discussion questions end each chapter.

Presbyterian Beliefs: A Brief Introduction. Donald K. McKim. Louisville, KY: Geneva Press, 2003.

This is a nontechnical introduction to and overview of basic Presbyterian beliefs. The book is divided into three major sections: The God Who Reveals, Creates, and Guides; The Christ Who Saves People Like Us; and The Church, Where Faith Begins, Is Nourished, and Grows. Each chapter ends with discussion questions.

Presbyterian Creeds: A Guide to the Book of Confessions. Jack Rogers. Louisville, KY: Westminster John Knox Press, 1991.

This book is an in-depth commentary on our *Book of Confessions.* Each confession is set in its historical context, and a thorough commentary provides interpretation on the confession's meaning today.

Presbyterian Questions, Presbyterian Answers: Exploring Christian Faith. Donald K. McKim. Louisville, KY: Geneva Press, 2004.

Using a question-answer format, the author tackles questions over a broad range of topics and answers each in a clear, understandable way from the heritage of Presbyterian confessions, polity, and practice. Sections include Presbyterian history, Bible, God, Jesus, humanity, Holy Spirit, salvation, church, and many more. This text can be used for individual study or can be easily adapted as a curriculum to cover basic Presbyterian beliefs. Also see *More Presbyterian Questions, More*

Presbyterian Answers by Donald K. McKim (Louisville, KY: Geneva Press, 2011), which includes more topics and answers.

Presbyterians: People of the Middle Way. Harry S. Hassal. Franklin, TN: Providence House Publishers, 1996.

Originally developed for new members' classes at Highland Park Presbyterian almost twenty years ago, this two-book set (student text and teacher's guide) still provides a simple but comprehensive introduction to what it means to be Presbyterian. The summaries and outlines provide accessible explanations of our history, beliefs, and practices. Can be easily adapted for leader training.

CPSIA information can be obtained
at www.ICGtesting.com
Printed in the USA
LVHW021039080522
717962LV00011B/130